PIONEER GROCERS OF ALASKA

Juneau in the 20th Century

By Marsha Erwin Bennett

To Barbara + Frank —
Enjoy the memories —
Love S Bennett
Marsha

PIONEER GROCERS OF ALASKA:
JUNEAU IN THE 20TH CENTURY

© 2015 by Marsha Erwin Bennett

ISBN 978-0-692-52297-4

Printed in Ashland, Oregon , United States of America
by Independent Printing Company

Cover design by Shawn Shaffer
Text design and layout by Kathy Munsel

Cover photos:
Marshall and Vivian Erwin in Case Lot Grocery
Bill Cope and salesman in 20th Century Supermarket
Bob Thibodeau in Bob's Shop-Rite Market

— printed on Recycled paper —

Dedication

This book is dedicated to my family—the Erwins— who over three generations kept a number of enterprises going for over 70 years.

FEATURED WRITERS/INTERVIEWS/ PHOTO CONTRIBUTORS

20ᵀᴴ CENTURY SUPERMARKET, FOODLAND	Gary Cope, Hub Sturrock Tim Whiting, Gary Paul
CASE LOT GROCERY, ERWIN'S GLACIER VILLAGE IGA	Vivian Erwin Renshaw Linda Erwin Androes Gene Erwin, Troy Erwin Jerry Rasler, Donna Hanna Barton
THIBODEAU'S MARKET, SALLY'S KITCHEN THIBODEAU LIQUOR STORES, BOB'S SHOP-RITE MARKET	Sally Thibodeau Paul Thibodeau Bob Thibodeau
HOME GROCERY	Hub Sturrock Bob Thibodeau Jack Hermle Jr
BM BEHRENDS, CALIFORNIA GROCERY	Hub Sturrock
RAINBOW FOODS	Dave Otteson
JUNEAU COLD STORAGE JUNEAU BUSINESS COMMUNITY	Elton Engstrom. Jr.
GASTINEAU GROCERY	Gary Paul
DEHART'S	Sandra DeHart Meehan

Interviews conducted by Marsha Erwin Bennett

Additional sources of information include R.N. DeArmond, digitalbob, Juneau Old Gold: Historical Vignettes of Juneau, Alaska, Compiled by R. N. DeArmond, Gastineau Historical Society, 1985, revised 1997.

Original interviews and submissions will be available at the Juneau-Douglas City Museum on project completion.

Table of Contents

Acknowledgment

Ten years ago this project began with days and weeks at the Alaska State Library, reading and copying microfiche files of Juneau newspapers, perusing Digital Bob, Bob DeArmond's many musings on historical details of early Juneau, and looking at old photos of grocery stores present from about 1930 to the 1960's, when Juneau assumed the role of State Capital of a new State of Alaska.

Like many others in Juneau, I started mining the stories of early pioneers in three volumes of the Pioneer Book Committee's Gastineau Memories. I asked friends and former Case Lot and Erwin's grocery employees for their stories. And I started slowly widening the circle of contacts among employees and owners of my parents' competitors in the early grocery trade.

Ten years later the stories, photos and ads have finally come together. I am proud of all the effort so many contributors made to this publication. Stories, autobiographies, photos, anecdotes all add up to a feeling and taste of what the old time grocery trade was like. You can feel the passion and dedication of folks trying to bring the best food they could to a small isolated town dependent on shipping that was not perfectly regular, during wartime. They were also volunteer firemen, club and city volunteers, parents and grandparents, church and city leaders. Juneau was small, between 5,000 and 8,000 residents before statehood.

Members of Gastineau Historical Society, especially Ginny Whitehead Breeze, Mike Blackwell and Marie Darlin contributed time and research or photos to this effort. Tim Whiting shared his autobiography which he had recently written for his grandchildren. Ralph Swap, Jerry Rasler, Donna Hanna Barton, Troy Erwin, Linda Erwin Androes and Kathy Munsel all added to the Case Lot-Erwin story with anecdotes, photos, and clarifications. Sally and Paul Thibodeau shared family photos and stories of Sally and Ken Thibodeau's grocery. Therese Thibodeau sent me the photo of her dad, Bob Thibodeau, more than once. Bob's long interview and emails to his family helped me understand the interplay of salesmen, grocers and trends over the years.

Gary Cope and Gary Paul gave me photos and commentary about 20th Century Market, early and late Foodland operations and personnel. John Hermle Jr. spent an evening with me showing his photos of the early Home Grocery and talking about his work there. Marlene Johnson, Al Kookesh, Sandra DeHart Meehan and Elton Engstrom, Jr. broadened the conversation to relationships beyond Juneau to Auke Bay and other SE Alaska towns and their local groceries.

With so many authors and contributors, editors have been important too. Anne Grisham Schultz was the first to organize the material. Mary Lou Gerbi refined later versions. Finally my niece Kathy Munsel, our own family historian, took on the final task of preparing the manuscript for printing. She also did a terrific job of taking old family photos and turning them into book-quality. Many friends and family members read drafts, as did most of the contributors or their family members.

I am grateful to the Alaska State Library for assistance, photos and encouragement. Staff at Juneau's City Museum have been very helpful too. Since moving to Ashland Judy Drais' writing class through OLLI, a program for retirees, helped me focus on finishing the project. Willamette Writers of South Oregon has been supportive too. One presentation in particular, by Midge Raymond of Ashland has been very helpful.

Finally, Shawn Shaffer completed the cover design and aided in finalizing the document for printing. I want to thank him and Frank Hutchinson at Independent Printing Company here in Ashland for their kind assistance.

Of course, I am responsible for all errors and omissions. I hope you enjoy the book. Marsha Erwin Bennett, September, 2015.

Introduction

The community of Juneau has only existed since about 1880. Indigenous Tlingit Indians settled in the area of what is now Tongass National Forrest hundreds to thousands of years earlier. A vast conifer forest, rich hunting and fishing resources and a site between mountains and glaciers nourished and maintained a few thousand native Tlingit from Seattle to Yakutat until the Gold Rush. Sitka to the south began as a Russian Fort for the harvesting of sea otter pelts, and grew as Russia's unofficial Capital City until the U.S. bought Alaska from Russia in1867. As Juneau grew with the discovery of gold, the Alaska Territorial Capital moved to Juneau in 1912, following an act of Congress.

In about 1880 gold miners discovered gold at Gold Creek in what is now downtown Juneau. A pair of prospectors, Joe Juneau and Frank Harris were led to the discovery by a Tlingit Elder, Kowee. Soon, both Douglas Island and the Juneau town site began to take shape as trees were cleared and tents sprang up. Over time gold mining on both sides of Gastineau Channel combined with a healthy fishing industry sustained both miners and their families and native Tlingit living in the area.

Miners from San Francisco and across America flocked to Juneau and Skagway in search of gold and what they hoped would be instant riches. Corporate mining followed the early "gold rush" in Juneau, Douglas and up the Chilkoot Trail to the Klondike. Suppliers in Juneau and Sitka supplied these early adventurers. A number of mining companies came and went until Treadwell mine in Douglas and later Alaska-Juneau Mine in Juneau began producing record quantities of gold in the area. Treadwell mine closed after an explosion flooded the mine. The Alaska Juneau continued until 1944 when gold prices made the mine unprofitable. (See David and Brenda Stone, Hard Rock Gold, 1980).

The Treadwell mine had a sizable footprint which included housing for the miners and their families, a recreation center, pool, library and mess halls. In Juneau, the Alaska-Juneau mine allowed for more entrepreneurship in the build-up of the Juneau site.

The first tents and cabins appeared on the hillside between Seward and Franklin Streets. Boats landed at high tide on the beach at what would become Front Street. Eventually planked sidewalks and streets hid the mud. Desperate for space, merchants perched their buildings on pilings over the water until that area was filled with crushed rock or "tailings" from the hard rock mines in later years.

Until 1945, the economies of Douglas and Juneau (the current City and Borough of Juneau) were dominated by these two mines. Logging, fishing and a few Territorial Government offices and private professionals rounded out the workforce in addition to a few local retail stores and restaurants. Over time Juneau's location as the seat of Territorial Government allowed for modest increases in population and services.

Most of our attention in this book concerns the 1930's-1960's before the town grew with statehood, and groceries were locally owned.

In 1959 Juneau became the capital of the new State of Alaska, Juneau's government offices mushroomed, with State, Federal and City government growing substantially and often filling up space in the downtown area. Soon corporate supermarkets found the growing capital city irresistible. The era of fierce competition between Juneau merchants was short-lived as first Fred Meyer and later K-Mart, Costco and Safeway took over the competition. Walmart occupied the K-Mart store building in the early new century. Today only Superbear in the Mendenhall Valley and Rainbow Foods downtown are locally owned supermarkets. Dehart's continues as a small general store in Auke Bay.

Economies of scale played a part in the location of the big stores in Juneau, as Native Land Claims were settled and the giant Prudhoe Bay oil find led to expansion of the oil industry and related services in Anchorage, Fairbanks and Kenai. Adding a store in Juneau was easier once corporate stores dotted neighborhoods in Anchorage and along the road system in Southcentral Alaska. The growth of the oil industry brought lobbyists, legislators, Native Corporations and non-profit organizations to town, as well as additional Federal, State and local government functions.

Air traffic evolved after World War II to include jets connecting Seattle and Anchorage, Juneau and Fairbanks and supplementing small local air services. A major road, The Alaska Highway, was built during the war in recognition of Alaska's strategic location. Refrigerated vans joined the growing barge traffic north in the 1960's.

State ferries came after statehood offering freight and passenger service between Washington, Prince Rupert and Alaska towns from Ketchikan to Skagway. Tourism grew as the Alaska Marine Highway expanded. Cruise ships began to dominate the tourism industry in the 1980's. Now close to one million tourists come to Juneau via cruise ship, ferry or jet during the summer months.

Early Grocers

Table 1 shows that already in 1881-82 the Northwest Trading Company operated in Juneau. By 1891, B.M. Behrends Department store and grocery occupied a large concrete structure on Seward Street. The building still provides space for local enterprises, including REACH, a local non-profit organization.

China Joe, the baker, came to Juneau in 1881, built a cabin at the corner of Third and Main Streets and operated his bakery there for 36 years. China Joe was the only Chinese man in Juneau for twenty years after Treadwell miners escorted all the other Chinese workers out of town. (R.N.DeArmond, The Founding of Juneau, 1967 and Nancy Ferrell, The Founding of Juneau, Alaska, 2008 and Alaska State Library, China Joe papers ca. 1917-2004)

Customer service was paramount for Juneau merchants at the time. The Decker Brothers general store advertised "Goods delivered free of charge by canoe or wheelbarrow." (Old Gold, p. 41)

Behrends Department Store dominated the food business in Juneau until 1908 when Mike George opened the first of several George Brothers groceries—this one in Douglas. The George brothers owned several businesses in the Juneau-Douglas area, over a period of 30 years. George Brothers' Pay N Takit and Leader Department store were located on Front Street and Ferry Way in 1917. In 1934 George changed his business to cash and carry, selling off most of the other merchandise and concentrating on groceries.

Bakeries, meat markets and coffee shops supplemented these early general stores. In 1914 Reliable Cash Grocery, Charles Goldstein's Emporium and Treadwell General Store all opened their doors to the growing population of the area.

Dozens of small stores followed during the 1920's and into the 1930's.

Piggly Wiggly, a national affiliate of an early American supermarket chain, opened in 1928 and continued here into the 1950's. This store was the training ground for several local men who went on to own their own grocery or manage a local store. Bert McDowell, Hub Sturrock, and Cliff Swap all worked there. Bert's Cash Grocery (1935), Home Grocery (1936) and Case Lot Grocery (1938) all benefited from Piggly Wiggly staff training. Treadwell Market in Douglas helped Sam Paul gain the experience he needed to join his brother Gabe in establishing Gastineau Grocery in 1927. The Paul family has continued in both wholesale and retail groceries and sales down to the last team of owners of Foodland in the 1990's.

By the 1930's many small groceries had come and gone. These early years, including World War I and the Depression found many small businesses started by men and women with little previous business experience. Others consolidated to meet changing demands. In 1937 Piggly Wiggly changed local owners and bought Sanitary Meat Company. In 1938 they absorbed United Food Company. The store changed hands again in 1951.

Bert McDowell's grocery started in 1935 on Willoughby Avenue, where Centennial Hall is now. Bert later moved the business to 211 Seward Street. When he sold out and became Mayor of Juneau in the early 1950's he sold to Bill Cope, surviving owner of the 20th Century Supermarket. His inventory became the seed of what was to become Foodland on Willoughby Avenue.

Nick Bavard was another early grocer who bought out Totem Grocery on Willoughby in 1935, renamed it California Grocery and moved the store location to South Franklin Street. Bavard's store was famous for its local fruits and vegetables, often grown in Bavard's garden in Auke Bay. He operated the business on South Franklin Street until he retired in the 1950's.

Irving's Grocery replaced Totem Grocery on Willoughby in 1935. Wilbur Irving, a flamboyant businessman from Cordova, also ran Whing-Ding's Night Club until it burned down. At about the same time (1945) Ron Capstead and Harold Bates bought his inventory and opened Juneau's first modern supermarket, 20th Century Supermarket, on Front and Seward Streets. These early supermarket pioneers had the vision and the skills to operate a much more advanced store than could be found in Juneau at the time. Their ads urged customers to come in to the store, pay cash and save. They were the first supermarket in Alaska, according to their ads. Their meat market was well known in town, they advertised on local radio, they built a parking lot for their customers later in the 1950's. They started a local tradition of give-aways including boats, airplane tickets and other prizes which have carried forward in one form or another in Juneau to this day.

In 1951 Harold Bates died in an airplane crash. His partner at the time, Bill Cope, continued to expand the business, opening Foodland Supermarket in 1953.

Harbor Market on 10th Street past what is now the Federal Building, opened in 1942 and operated as a neighborhood market into the 1950's. It was first owned by the Nygards, later sold to Frieda and Andy Robinson in the 1950's. When Glacier Village IGA opened, Marshall and Vivian Erwin bought Robinson's inventory. Frieda came to work for the Erwins at their new airport location. Andy opened a men's store in the new shopping center, later known as Airport Shopping Center. Their son, Charles, eventually purchased the grocery business from Vivian Erwin after Marshall's death in 1973. He had been Erwin's accountant and a partner in Erwin's

Glacier Village IGA prior to buying the IGA store at Airport Shopping Center and the new store, later named SuperBear, at Mendenhall Mall. SuperBear is now the only locally owned Supermarket in the Juneau area.

Family Businesses to Corporate Structure

Because of their physical isolation from Lower 48 markets and trends, most Juneau grocery stores remained small family-owned operations located downtown in the 1930s and 1940s, gradually moving to the Mendenhall valley in the 1950s and 1960s. Employees took orders over the phone, selected the merchandise and delivered it to people's homes or apartments. Business was personal.

Eventually, however, the history of Juneau's grocery stores paralleled the global transformation of small-scale retail businesses to corporate giants. But Juneau's changes started much later. Major changes in the grocery business in the Lower 48 states accelerated with the spread of the Great Atlantic and Pacific Tea Company (A&P) and other smaller "chain" stores. By 1930, A&P operated 16,000 stores in 34 states and two Canadian provinces. (Marc Levinson, The Great A&P and the Struggle for Small Business in America, 2011). But like Piggly Wiggly, A & P eventually died out once its owners passed away. In both cases the managers who followed were unable to sustain the energy and drive of its founders.

Although national trends took time to appear in Juneau, Juneau's small grocery merchants also underwent what Levinson calls "creative destruction," the demise of the "mom-n-pop-shop" and the rise of corporate conglomerates. From at least twenty small grocery stores, meat markets and bakeries, the Juneau grocery scene gradually transformed into a local scaled-back variation of the national retail trend with a few giant retail behemoths. Consumers traded the personal connections and interdependency of the small shops so they could get variety of goods, reduced cost and fresher foods from the corporate stores.

The trend from local to global started slowly in Juneau. In the early 1930s, Piggly Wiggly was Juneau's only "chain" store, lasting into the early '50s when the Ben Franklin store took over their location on Front Street. Like many other Lower 48 companies that attempted to garner the Juneau market, Piggly Wiggly's owners chose to go elsewhere after two decades here.

Substantial changes in Juneau grocery retailing came in 1945 with the opening of the 20th Century Super Market on Front Street, one of the first cash-and-carry stores. In 1953, Foodland opened on Willoughby Avenue. Both downtown stores had large parking lots, were centrally located downtown and operated as corporations with an influx of changing owners. During the 1950s and 1960s, the 20th Century store expanded and modernized while many of the other small grocery stores closed or moved away. In 1963, Foodland burned down, but the owners rebuilt a bigger and nicer store (twice, according to Gary Cope) and went on to dominate shopping in downtown Juneau until they sold to another Alaska grocery chain, Alaskan and Proud, in 1995.

A Juneau couple, Marshall and Vivian Erwin, went through the changes from small-family business to corporate structure and supermarket variety during the 1930s to 1960s. Case Lot Grocery, located on the waterfront at South Franklin Street, opened in 1938 as the Erwin's family-owned grocery store. The Erwins and their employees delivered groceries to Juneau residents, including many Alaska Native customers, supplied fishing boats and served as a wholesaler for Alaska Native village stores throughout southeast Alaska. As times changed, the family remodeled their store to Erwin's Supermarket in the 1950s and incorporated.

In 1963, the Erwins developed a new store and gas station in the airport area. Glacier Village IGA, the first supermarket in the growing Mendenhall Valley, which was later connected with Juneau's first shopping mall, the Airport Shopping Center, at the intersection of Shell Simmons Drive and Glacier Highway near the airport. Alaska Native carvings graced the storefront and walls of the building. The Erwins closed their downtown Erwin's Supermarket store in 1967 after moving to the airport location 5 years earlier. Erwin's Glacier Village IGA was sold to Charlie Robinson and others in 1978. Following the sale, the store became Shop N Kart and later Family Grocer. Alaska Industrial Hardware, an Anchorage-based company with stores throughout the Northwest and Alaska, operates there now.

The Thibodeau family has been a continual presence in Juneau grocery and liquor businesses in Juneau. Founded by Joe Thibodeau and his partner, John Hermle, in 1926, Home Grocery has continued through the Thibodeau family's enterprises to its present form. Bob Thibodeau worked for his father, Joe as a young teenager, later was a salesman and owned his own grocery in Douglas for many years. His brother Ken took over the grocery from Joe and John. Ken's son now owns 4 local neighborhood liquor stores in the Juneau area. Sally's Kitchen continues Sally and Ken's successful delicatessen business.

The pattern of family-to-corporate ownership was typical of other successful grocery stores in Alaska, such as Larry Carr's family-owned Carr's Quality Center stores, which started in a Quonset hut in Anchorage. Carr and partner Barney Gottstein developed stores throughout Alaska before selling to Safeway, North America's second-largest supermarket chain.

By 1983 with the entry of Portland, Ore., food giant, Fred Meyer, a division of Kroger International, Juneau retail soon became dominated by supermarket chains, including Safeway, Costco and Kmart, later Wal-Mart stores. All of these stores are centrally controlled, heavily bureaucratic and standard-ized giant corporations. They provide most of Juneau's food and other retail merchandise and dominate most local and regional markets worldwide.

These big-box super-sized stores have their own distribu-tion systems, supply chains and huge offerings of food and other consumer staples. Wal-Mart is the global leader in the food business, largest private employer in the world. Other big-box stores are part of huge multinational corporations, either growing from a single store, like Wal-Mart and ear-lier A & P, or consolidations of regional market stores now sharing their new owner's name and products. (Fred Mey-er). Safeway has grown through similar acquisitions. Whole Foods is now a nationally based supermarket growing both in new locations and through acquisitions of other estab-lished Health Food stores. Costco was founded in Seattle and has recently expanded nationally and into international markets as well.

Although corporate stores have dominated Juneau retail in recent years, well-established firms continue to compete and thrive. David Otteson's Rainbow Foods natural -organic food store typifies a counter trend toward more personal service and the eat-healthy-and-buy local movement. This Juneau "niche" player has brought back some of the personal style and com-munity once dominant in Juneau, along with organic foods, natural vitamins and delicious lunches and specialty dinners.

DeHarts in Auke Bay is another "niche" player in the Juneau area, with a long history serving customers and fishermen. Jim and Jane DeHart opened their Auke Bay neighborhood grocery in 1941. They moved the store to its present location in 1946, adding a gas station and marina in 1955. According to the DeHarts, Auke Bay had only 35 homes, all but one without electricity, in 1941. The store used glacier ice to cool cans of pop for their customers. The groceries, liquor, gas and marina have become a stable part of the growing Auke Bay community into the 21st Century. The business has new owners but still maintains the original DeHart family name.

A Tapestry of Interviews

The story of Juneau grocers is a small tapestry at first, composed of interviews and submissions from local grocers, their children or employees. The key players are grocers, their families and their employees—from box boys to managers to owners, who tell their stories through interviews and their own stories collected from 2004 to 2007.

Most of these businesses had similar ways of doing business. Overlapping statements emphasize that stores had similar practices due to the technology of the time. Researched stories and advertisements from the Juneau Empire and other publications of the era fill in the gaps. Photos come from a variety of sources, including family photos and State of Alaska historical photo collections. Chapters are organized by theme.

The voices represent individuals in some of Juneau's grocery businesses operating here during the 20th century. I hope these stories create a picture of Juneau families buying and using their groceries, of some of the perils and pleasures of the business at that time and of the cooperation and community spirit that prevailed in those early days.

The approach is more Sociology than history. Juneau families and businesses worked together in a cooperative enterprise that worked during the hard times before and after gold mining stopped supporting the town. Juneau is still an isolated place. Many of the traditions we share today started in the early years before World War II. Maybe that is why so many of us continue to choose to live here.

CANADIAN
EGGS
2 doz. for 1.19

1

EARLY GARDEN
PEAS
2 cans 25¢

Very Personal Service

Hub Sturrock, who started working for B. M. Behrend's Department Store in the grocery department in 1936, retired 48 years later as one of the owners of Foodland Supermarket. Sturrock discusses B. M. Behrend's Department Store orders and deliveries during the 1930s.

Shortly after high school I went to work in the grocery department of the B.M. Behrend's Department Store at Third and Seward Streets. Customers could shop in the store or call in their orders by telephone to "5," which was one of Juneau's first business phone numbers. Most people charged their groceries and were billed once per month. Clerks set up the orders, placing them in boxes for delivery, usually made three times a day. The boxes were wood with metal hinges that were collapsible for easy storage. Nobody locked their doors in those days. Deliverymen often put frozen items in the freezer and perishables in the refrigerator or icebox. Many apartments had small closets, less than waist high, by the front door of each apartment. Deliveries were made to those closets. Stores also took orders from people who lived in outlying communities. There were small freighters that went from Juneau to Hoonah and other villages once a week. Two of them were the Estebeth and the Yakobi. Grocery stores were everywhere. By the late 1930s there were as many as twenty grocery stores in Juneau.

Hub Sturrock's List of Grocery Stores in Juneau with date founded

1892   B. M. Behrend's, B. M. Behrend owner
239 Seward, corner of Third
Closed 1957; formerly Sitka Trading Co. 1887-1891

1908   **George Bros. Market** (Joe, Gus, & Tom),
Gus owned Superette Market, Bros the liquor store
1946   S. Franklin & Ferry Way

1909   **Izzy Goldstein's Supply**, Izzy Goldstein owner
251 So. Franklin

1914   **United Food Co. (**Built 1914, remodeled 1935)
Front Street, moved to Goldstein Bldg,
125 Seward St

1920's Washington Cooperative
Fourth & Main, next to Fire Hall
Miners' co-op

1926   **Home Grocery**, (formerly Totem Grocery)
John Hermle & Joe Thibodeau owners
Gold Creek Bridge on Willoughby

1928   **Piggly Wiggly**
Front St, in Percy Reynold's Bldg.

        Blomgren's Market
Front St., next to Nance's Dime Store

1933   **Cottage Food Store**, Fred Martin and
Wilbur Irving? owners
142 Willoughby (now Centennial Hall)

1935   **Bert's Cash Grocery**
Bert McDowell owner
224 Seward, same side as Behrend's

        Thibodeau's Market, Joe Thibodeau owner
Willoughby Avenue (now Fireweed Place)

1936 **California Grocery**, Nick Bavard owner
South Franklin, across from Decker Bldg @233

1937 **Gastineau Grocery**, Sam Paul owner
Front St., across from 20th Century Market

1938 **Case Lot Grocery,** (became Erwin's Supermarket)
Marshall & Vivian Erwin owners
240 So. Franklin

Jim Ellen's
Willoughby

1942 **Garnick's Grocery**
127 Seward St., across from Behrend's
22 yrs. in business.

1945 **20th Century Market**, Bill Cope owner
142 Front St (corner of Seward)
First National Bank in 1899, recently McDonald's

1953 **Thibodeau's Market**,
Ken and Sally Thibodeau owners
Willoughby Avenue

1950's **Glover's Spruce Market**,
Al Glover and Les Sturm owners
Glacier Highway at the foot of Tenth Street
Lockers for fish and game

1978 **Home Grocery & Liquor,**
Ken and Sally Thibodeau owners
Whittier Street

Source: Hub Sturrock, plus additional information from Alaska State Library Historical Collection, compiled by Captain Lloyd H. "Kinky" Bayers, Juneau Historical Subject Files. Additional information from Vivian Erwin Renshaw and Marie Darlin, Gastineau Historical Society.

Gene Erwin, nephew of Case Lot grocery and Glacier Village IGA founders Marshall and Vivian Erwin, describes Case Lot Grocery Store deliveries in the 1940s:

There were no supermarkets then [1944]. Almost all the groceries were bought monthly, according to the agreement. The store was open from 7 am until 6 pm and closed on Sundays. Customers called their orders in on the phone. We would write the order on order blanks and became quite good at grocer's shorthand. TP was toilet paper. XXX was powdered sugar…. Once the order was filled and placed in delivery boxes, the boxes were lined up in the back to be delivered. The deliveryman, (me) for a lot of the time I worked there, would load them in a one-ton panel truck in the order of delivery. Delivering the groceries could get real interesting. We were always pushed for time and would rush up to a door, tap twice and walk right in. No one locked doors in those days. Sometimes our customers would not be ready for visitors, but we just said, "Good morning," unloaded the groceries, and rushed right out. If no one was home, which was most of the time, we would put milk and other perishables in the refrigerator, if there was one. I remember a dear lady who lived up seven flights of stairs who would order just a few things every day so I wouldn't have too much to carry. She meant well! Another, who lived way up on Starr Hill, would only order once a month so I wouldn't have to make so many trips. Sometimes her grocery boxes weighed over 100 pounds, and if she ordered a case of canned milk and 25 pounds of flour, it meant two trips. She meant well, too!

A lot of our business was shipped to customers living where there were no stores. We would get a letter listing what was wanted and we would fill the order. Much of it was not carried in our store, but Clifford Swap, our manager, would go all over town to fill it [the order], if it was available. These orders were carefully packed for shipping and delivered to the Yakobi, an ex-halibut boat. The *Yakobi* was the mail boat, too, so it sailed regardless of the weather. Sometimes it would come in so iced down you wondered how it stayed afloat.

Tim Whiting, who began working as a fourteen-year-old "box boy" at Erwin's downtown store, also talks about Case Lot Grocery Store deliveries:

This was not your two-bag delivery. In those days the large Filipino and Native community as well as many others shopped by the month. Many had veteran's or social security checks that came once a month and they spent it all on groceries. Many families did not have cars and delivery was the way groceries got home. They bought 100 pound bags of rice, potatoes, cases of evaporated milk, 50-pound bags of flour, etc., and most of these [customers] lived up as many as ten flights of stairs, a good reason to have groceries delivered. The store delivered once a day Monday-Wednesday and twice a day or more as needed on Thursday-Saturday. Cashiers would write down name, address, number of boxes and time of preferred delivery. The deliveryman would collect the slips and then "route" the deliveries in such a manner that you never had to backtrack throughout the delivery. You learned every street, alley, stairway, apartment building and customer preference real quick or you would never finish your deliveries in time.

Groceries were put into collapsible wooden crates that were loaded and placed in the warehouse until time for delivery. You walked in [the house] and unloaded the boxes, placing frozen and cooler items in the refrigerator, the rest on a counter and took the boxes with you. About half of the time no one was home when you delivered, and I never remember an incident of theft concerning a delivery person from any of the stores in town, but generally the delivery person was a long-term employee. Occasionally the person or persons in the house would be preoccupied and would not hear you come in. This made for some interesting stories.

One that happened to me concerned a young preacher's wife who was extremely good looking and always had the male help at Erwin's Market on their toes when she shopped. I was 18 and delivering for Erwin's and had been at their house several times. They were hardly ever home when I delivered. I knocked on the door, yelled "Groceries," and entered the long hallway that led to their kitchen, going past several closed doors in the process. After carrying in three large boxes of groceries, I knelt down to take the refrigerated items out of the boxes and heard a door open behind me. I assumed it was the front door opening and I turned around to identify myself when the preacher's wife stepped out of a bathroom drying herself off with a towel. She screamed, I screamed, she screamed [again] and ran into the bathroom. I screamed and ran out the front door totally embarrassed and thankful at the same time. I never said a word to anyone at the store because I was sure no one would believe me, and I didn't want to embarrass her further, but I didn't need to worry as she evidently began doing her shopping elsewhere.

When the winter storms would come, everyone would have their groceries delivered. The worse it got, the more deliveries you would have. There was also the convenience of calling in your order and having it delivered, so when no one wanted to leave home in the storm, they would call and have it delivered. I can remember going up Gastineau Avenue in two ruts that would throw you all over to get to the abandoned Home Hotel at the end and then packing groceries through the snow drifts along the side of the deserted hotel to reach the State Apartments at the top of stairs that ran from South Franklin to Gastineau Avenue level. They were inaccessible from below because snow drifted over the eight flights of stairs. I don't ever remember a time that customers were told that the weather was so bad we couldn't deliver.

Deliverymen did not like making a lot of trips up stairs and into houses so they always wanted the boxes as full and as heavy as possible. We had a big guy named Mike Overman who could pack anything you put on him, and he was constantly telling us boxers to make them [the boxes] heavier so he wouldn't have to make so many trips. The delivery boxes in those days were collapsible wooden boxes that were reusable. There was one size, extra large. One day he got on us, so while he was making his morning delivery, we took the groceries out of a large wooden delivery box and nailed it to the floor (the warehouse had all wooden floors); placed a note in the bottom that said, "Heavy enough for you"; put the groceries back in and left. He just about tore his arms out of the socket when he went to throw that box into the delivery truck. He was not amused.

While delivering nights when snow and wind created drifts and slippery roads, it was accepted practice by delivery people and taxis, who as a general rule were the only ones out in the weather, to use local knowledge of which streets you could get up and which hills needed a two- or three-block run to make it up. As no one had four-wheel drive, we all used chains that would break and beat the hell out of the side of the truck sometimes when you could not stop. One of the tricks to making it up Starr Hill to Kennedy or above was to start your run at St. Ann's Hospital, which was two blocks from the bottom of the hill. Of course there were two stop signs along the way but by turning off your lights on the late run, you could see if someone was coming up the other way on the hills that intersected and stop or take evasive action before your paths crossed. We all used this trick until two cabs, one going across Sixth to make Starr Hill, and the other coming up Harris to make Basin Road, T-boned as both had their lights off.

Jerry Rasler, a delivery driver for Erwin's supermarket in the late 1950s, confirms that people trusted grocery store employees to enter their homes and put away groceries.

> Deliveries were usually made three times a day at ten, two and four. We also had to make box runs to the liquor stores and bars to collect empty boxes to pack groceries in. There was a lot of competition between the four stores for these. Delivery had not changed much since the early days. People still did not lock doors. You would knock, enter, unload groceries and go on to the next stop. Most people were not home, so we often put the perishables away for them.

Bob Thibodeau, whose father Joe Thibodeau joined John Hermle in the Home Grocery business from 1935 until 1940, remembers being a "swamper," helping deliver groceries during his time working at Home Grocery.

> In 1935 I was 13 years old and at that time most of the grocery stores operated on two principles: one was credit and the other was delivery service. In the delivery service, the driver, especially on weekends [Saturday],

needed a swamper who helped the driver to deliver the groceries to the various homes. Well, I was one. Every store had a swamper. There were a lot of small stores in Juneau at that time. The only one that operated on a cash basis was 20th Century Market—and that only occurred in 1945. Up until that time all the stores operated on a credit basis.

He [the swamper] carried the boxes of groceries up into the house and knocked on the door. A woman told me that…. Scotty, a fellow who worked for Kenny and I, would actually put the groceries into the refrigerator, and it was really a very personal service.

Generally there would be the driver and the swamper. The truck would stop, and there would be two or three orders to the various houses around, and they [the swamper] would chip in. It was quite a technique delivering groceries because the driver would have a list of deliveries he would have to make, and he would check them out, and he would stack the groceries so that he wasn't going to have to come back and forth. There was a route.

Well, if you had the [collapsible wooden] boxes you used them because they stacked well. The others [cardboard boxes] were odd sizes and didn't stack too well.

I was a salesman from 1949 to 1954. Coffee time was after the delivery truck went out. And so, I remember going down to Belle's Café almost every morning around 10:30 with Bert McDowell [Bert's Cash Grocery].

Elton Engstrom Sr., a Juneau business owner, remembers the special compartments built into homes for the delivery of groceries and other goods.

My wife and I in 1983 bought the Fosbee Apartments and this apartment building had been constructed in 1936. Each of these apartments had a little compartment built into the apartment that opened from the inside of the apartment and also opened from the outside of the apartment, and it was next to the door of the apartment. This little compartment was about 12 inches wide and 24 to 30 inches tall. It wasn't big, about the size of what you would imagine a dog kennel resembles.... It was for the grocery man when he brought the order to open that door and place it into the recess. And then when the customer came back to the apartment, they opened up the inside of the door and got the groceries out. That emphasizes the uniqueness of the trade then—that it was a very personal trade. It was a trade where people were buying on credit to a great extent and where people didn't go to the grocery stores. They called in their order and got what they wanted, which is so unique when you consider the shopping habits of today where people have to go to the store to see what they are buying.... There's no personal contact, so this was very much a personal relationship. [For example] the milk was delivered. Of course the fellow who later established the Nugget Department Store out at Nugget Mall was the milkman for many many years - Ron Flint.

2

The Customer's Perspective

By the early 1940's grocery carts and frozen food cases began appearing in local stores. Grocery carts didn't become common until aisles were wider and customers came to the store to shop for themselves.

Hub Sturrock mentioned that Behrends was a "Libby's store" for all canned goods. Later 20th Century Market featured Libby's brands. Case Lot bought S & W brands. Foodland featured the Western Family brand, as did Shop N Kart and SuperBear. Western Family, Kroger's, Fred Meyer and other "store" brands became much more common by the 1960's as customers became accustomed to the lower prices these brands offered.

Elton Engstrom, Jr:

> When my wife and I got married in the 1960s, we favored Kenny Thibodeau's store. I don't know why. All the stores had delivery trucks. My wife would call in her order and she'd say, "I want this and this and this," and the order would be delivered to the house. That was very unlike today where everyone has to go to the stores and has to buy their merchandise.

Bob Thibodeau:

> Katherine Shaw told me years afterwards—she was a customer of the Home Grocery and was a relative of

John Hermle—that all winter long she did not enter the store. All of her business was done over the phone. And the phone—that's what most of the women who worked in the Territory [the Territorial offices before Alaska became a state] or had jobs did. And most of the housewives, too. Why get out? Your women clerks—their job was to answer the phone and put up the orders. There would be a relationship between the customer and the phone person. So she [the employee on the phone] knew this particular head of lettuce was not up to her [customer's] standards. But this other woman, she didn't mind too much. She [the clerk] could get rid of that piece of lettuce without getting a complaint.

At the time there were relatively few home freezers. So if you were a person who fished and hunted, you got a locker. Juneau Cold Storage was the only place that gave that service. They devoted a whole big frozen area to the community. It had baskets in it and they would be open to the public.

If a person came in to shop, and it was a credit customer, then we would only use totals. We would ring it up in the register. There were only three different categories: there was produce, meat and everything else. We would give them [the customer] the tape. The [adding machine] tape would show a certain item was a dairy item, a certain item was groceries, or non-foods.

[About the grocery store's credit book and grocery carts]: My father didn't have a grocery cart. When Kenny [Thibodeau] started, he had maybe one or two grocery carts. You know, in most grocery stores, if a person—a customer—came into the store, she or he brought the item to a counter where the [counter] person would write it up. Everybody had a book. In my father's business, the customer had his own book [which listed what the customer owed].

My feeling is that in the early days grocery people were very special. They really wanted to help others. They would do almost anything for a customer. The customer was always right. If the customer wanted more credit, OK. Unless the customer complained about something, then it was OK.

I remember one time my brother had quite a number of Natives as customers. And with Native people you had to put a limit on how much they could charge. If you didn't, the bill would get out of bounds. So this one time, this one Native family, after a kin died, the son told me that his mother said to the dad, "We don't have any groceries. Go down to Kenny's and get some groceries." And he said, "We reached the limit." She responded, "Go down and do it anyway." At that time, Kenny wouldn't turn them down, but he would say that they could only get so much. So the woman was pregnant, and when the baby was born, she named him Kenny. (laughing) That kind of relationship existed between customers [and stores].

3

The Scene at the Stores

I n her essay, "The History of the Erwin Building," Vivian Erwin writes about the downtown building that housed the Case Lot Grocery for many years.

Vivian Erwin Renshaw:

The history of the Erwin Building is interwoven with the early history of my involvement in the grocery business. Charles Goldstein built the original building in 1928 on South Franklin Street next to Connor's Motors. It was first rented to Frank Harris who had a furniture store there (No relation to the original Juneau founder Harris or his family). Harris built two additional stories to the building in 1930. The second story was part warehouse and part display and "the third floor had six one-bedroom apartments finished in varnished plywood walls and ceiling and had coal stoves for heat. The hallway was not finished. Apparently (Harris) exhausted his funds and so Charles Goldstein was then the owner of a building more than twice the original size. In 1935 or 1936 a restaurant was opened in part of the front section of the building by Brownie and Joe Erwin, my future in-laws. It was a family-style restaurant and was very successful.

In 1938 we opened Case Lot Grocery in a small 14-by-28-foot area beside the restaurant. The rent was $35 per month. Our daughter Linda was five months old.

In 1941 the restaurant closed. Brownie and Joe had gone to manage the A-J Boarding House in the Gold Creek Basin and the new operators of the café were not good operators and soon closed it. We then enlarged the grocery store and leased the whole building from Mr. Goldstein for ten years at $100 per month. In just a few months Marshall had made plans to make extensive improvements to the building so he asked for an additional ten years on the lease, which was given at the increased rental of $125 per month. Mr. Cleveland at the Behrends Bank was really impressed that we got such a good deal from Mr. Goldstein.

Up until that time the store had been heated by a circulating heater in the front section and another in the back room to heat the warehouse. In the winter it was barely enough to keep the temperature above freezing as the tide came in and out under the building and the floors were wooden with many open spaces. We installed central heating, which was a great improvement. Marshall built the first produce refrigeration in the town and soon we were shipping produce to the outlying communities, even as far as Sitka.

In 1943 we closed the store and leased the first two floors to the Signal Corps of the Army for a supply depot. They quartered a contingent of troops, about 200 men, in the building. On Christmas Eve, in 1943, the Army returned the building to us. Since we had it leased, we had no alternative but to reopen the store. Marshall repainted the fixtures and built some new ones, and we prepared to open the store in the spring. We ordered the groceries and other supplies and announced our reopening the week before the A-J mine closed. Predictions were made that grass would grow in the streets, but it didn't happen. The business grew as fast as we could run and keep up with it. In 1955 on August 15, we purchased the building from Charles Goldstein for $40,000. After signing the papers we walked down to the building and saw the Juneau Cold Storage on fire (a few blocks south).

In 1956 we purchased the property next door that belonged to Izzy and Carol Goldstein and Minnie Goldstein. We tore down the Tenford Rooms and the cabins and filled the tidelands including the area underneath the building. We then doubled the size of the grocery store section, (and) made and paved the parking lot, the first one in the downtown area.

In 1957 in January, we opened Erwin's Supermarket with a new name and new mode of operation (cash and carry). We enclosed the stairway to the apartments and added additional warehouse space and refrigeration at the rear of the building (and) had a sprinkler system installed. In 1963 a fire was set in the stairway but the sprinkler put it out before the fire department even got there. A month or so later Foodland burned to the ground. (It didn't have a sprinkler system)

In 1964 we opened Glacier Village IGA (at the airport). In 1968 we closed Erwin's Supermarket. In November 1976 we sold the building to Mr. and Mrs. George Davidson who later sold it. (It has changed owners several times since then).

Vivian Erwin Renshaw's summary of her family's grocery business history sounds many of the same notes found in Dave Otteson's short history of Rainbow Foods.

David Otteson:

Natural foods burst onto the national scene in the early 1970s. My first experience with a natural food store came in 1977 when I was living in Washington, D.C.

There was a large natural food store near Georgetown (University) called Yes! (The exclamation point was part of the name). I remember walking into the place and thinking, "This is different."

I moved to Juneau in August 1978 and one of the first places I sought out was Season's Supply. It was a tiny health food store located upstairs in the "Mother Earth Mall," which is above where Heritage Coffee is today. There were two or three other stores up there including The Foggy Mountain Shop.

Sometime in late 1979 my wife, Mary Alice McKeen, learned that Shar (Smith) was looking for business partners because Season's Supply was going to move and expand. We invested $10,000 that Mary Alice had recently inherited and became shareholders with the idea that I would work at the store. The business was incorporated in January 1980 as Rainbow Foods.

Rainbow Foods opened on April 1, 1980. It was up-stairs in the old Alaska Steam Laundry Building, later called the Emporium Mall (on South Franklin Street), which was owned by the MacKinnon family. The original Rainbow Foods was about 1,000 square feet, more than twice the size of Seasons Supply. It was replete with wood fixtures that were typical of natural food stores at the time, including wooden bulk food bins. Of course, it didn't take us long to discover that wooden fixtures are utterly impractical for a food business because they are really hard to clean. On the first day of business our sales exceeded $500, which we considered a tremendous success.

While our business grew steadily in this location, there were some drawbacks. The biggest was being upstairs in a building that had no freight elevator. Every week we had to haul hundreds, and later thousands, of pounds of freight up a long stairway. It wasn't obvious to us how crazy this was until later when we moved to a street level and didn't have to do it anymore.

In 1985 we opened a second store in Jordan Creek Center in the [Mendenhall] valley across from Nugget Mall. Originally several successful downtown retailers were planning on going to Jordan Creek; however, right around that time oil prices tanked and the local economy collapsed. Everyone aborted their plans for a valley location except us. We found ourselves virtually alone in an empty mall. At the end of 1986, we closed the Jordan Creek store.

In early 1987, we moved out of the Emporium and opened our first "street-level" store at Second and Franklin. We were able to do this without too much expense because we still had all our fixtures from the Jordan Creek store. It was here that Rainbow first started doing food service. We made sandwiches, salad, soup, muffins and pizza every weekday in a tiny food prep area. We also made carrot juice. Cliff Nelson, who operated the juicer, tried to have a new joke every day for our customers. He reminded everyone who would listen that while the juice cost $2, the jokes were free.

The business thrived at its street-level location. This verified the old saying that the three most important things in retail are location, location, location. Now that people could see where we were, we got a lot more business. We moved (to a new location) in the Simpson building at Second and Seward in March of 1992.

The Simpson building location was almost twice as big. It provided the opportunity to have a larger kitchen and a lot more refrigeration and freezer capacity. The biggest expansion came in produce. We were able to triple the size of our produce department, going from carrying between 15 and 20 items to more than 50. To me, this made us a legitimate food store. Even though we were bigger, we were (and still are) a "niche" store, serving a particular segment of the population. Folks have sometimes asked me how Rainbow has remained successful since many of the products we sell are available at "mainstream" stores. The answer, as far as I can tell, is that our store appeals to a segment of the market that is devoted to a "natural lifestyle." The people who are our customers sense that we share their commitment to an approach to food and health. One way we do this is by having fairly stringent standards about what we will and will not carry in the store. A few years ago we converted our produce section to 100% organic.

We moved to 224 Fourth Street in August 2003. In April of 2005, Rainbow Foods celebrated its 25th Anniversary. The newest incarnation [of Rainbow Foods] was an immediate success. This was a tremendous relief because, like most remodeling projects, it cost more than anticipated. Being a smaller store has the advantage of letting you get to know your customers and employees on a more personal level. And since our customers share a common interest in good food and healthy living, there is a real sense of community. So it's been a nice thing to be a part of.

Foodland Supermarket

In 1955 The Daily Alaska Empire carried an eight-page spread heralding the new Foodland Supermarket, which opened August 25, 1955. It featured an architect's drawing of the building and listed all the managers of the departments with their pictures and a short biography for each of them. Congratulatory ads filled many of the following pages, from fellow businesses and the many contractors who built the building and supplied its fixtures.

The building was built by Stutte and Son and designed by Lynn Forest and Son Architects. The article stated, "Several salesmen looked it over, and they agreed that there might be some larger, but none more modern in design, construction and efficiency." The building was all-concrete except the roof, according to Walter Stutte.

Another column discussed Bill Cope, the owner. "The idea man behind the building of the store is Bill Cope, owner and manager. Cope was a manager of a store in St. Louis, Mo., but decided to come to Alaska because, as he said, 'There is no future there [in Missouri].' He came to Juneau in 1944 as a meat cutter for Bates and Capstead and went into partnership with Bates in 1948. Bates and Cope bought out the Foodland market from Bert McDowell in 1953. Harold Bates was killed in a plane crash in 1954, and under a partnership agreement, the business went to Cope."

The store had fixtures of the "most modern and sanitary design" and "the door to the building is [was] the first automatically opening door in Juneau. Their parking lot, the largest in southeast Alaska at over 10,000 square feet, was designed to handle at least 150 cars at a time. Walter and Bob Stutte owned the land and the buildings but leased them to Foodland on long-term leases. [Herman] Smokey Rosenberger, a ten-year employee of 20th Century Super Market, became Foodland's new manager. (Source: Gary Cope)

Just one year earlier, July 1954, an ad thanking Alaska Steamship Company appeared in The Daily Alaska Empire. E. L. Reed of Sitka mentioned "Your company is to be commended for the initiation of unitized cargo to the Territory. The day of dirty and torn flour and sugar sacks, dented cans, and leaking bottles has passed. (may it never return)...pilferage is now confined to those items not unitized... checking is easier."

By the time Foodland opened the next year, not only were the store and fixtures new, but the food shipped was generations better than had ever been available in Juneau.

Back in 1936 when Hub Sturrock went to work for Behrend's Department Store, he climbed a ladder behind the counter and used a fishing pole to bring down cans from the high shelves. Freight came in once a week via Alaska Steamship Line. In later years, Northland Transportation and Lyndon Transport provided this service. Behrend's store was one long room with two aisles for the grocery department and the rest of the store—dry goods, department store, shoes, linoleum, everything." By 1955 it was a "whole new ballgame" in Juneau.

Early Grocers

Behrend's Store in the 1910s or 20s. Alaska State Library #P87-1028, Winter & Pond collection.

Hub Sturrock went to work in the grocery department of B.M. Beherends right out of high school in 1936. Sue Judson collection.

California Grocery, in the early 1920s. Alaska State Library #P109-73, Katherine Shaw photograph collection.

A California Grocery delivery truck in front of their store on South Franklin St., 1920s or early 1930s. Alaska State Library #P87-1040, Winter & Pond collection.

George Brother's Grocery Department, in the early 1930s. Alaska State Library #P87-1038, Winter & Pond collection.

Sam Paul Sr., Sam Paul Jr., Bud Whiteside and an unidentified man stand in front of the Gastineau Grocery, which opened in 1937. Gary Paul collection.

A collection of wooden grocery boxes from early Juneau Stores.
Photo by Marie Darlin.

*Case Lot Grocery storefront in the early 1940s, South Franklin St.
Erwin family collection.*

*Vivian Erwin, daughters, Marsha (in stroller) and Linda, in front of a Case Lot
Grocery delivery truck in 1942. The stairs on the right lead to the apartments
above the store where the family lived and rented out for extra income.
Kathy Munsel collection.*

Marshall and Vivian Erwin surrounded by produce, 1949 Case Lot Grocery. Erwin family collection.

Marshall Erwin, owner of Case Lot Grocery, stands proudly in front of his new Miracle Whip display. Erwin family collection

20th Anniversary, 1957, Case Lot Grocery, Erwin's Supermarket. Erwin family collection.

Esther Godkin Jokala, cashier, 1956. Erwin family collection.

Cliff Swap at work in the Case Lot Grocery store, 1950's. Erwin family collection.

Gene Erwin, 1950's.
Kathy Munsel collection.

Linda Erwin, 1955.
Kathy Munsel collection.

Vivian Erwin, Frieda Robinson and Marshall Erwin working in the crowded Erwin's Supermarket Office in 1959. Kathy Munsel collection.

The first King Crab to arrive in a Juneau grocery store were brought in by Marshall Erwin from Cordova and offered to the customers of Erwin's Supermarket. Joseph Alexander Photo, 1968.

Erwin's Supermarket customers, 1957. Kathy Munsel collection.

Erwin's Glacier Villiage entrance, 1964. The handsome building faced Lemon Glacier, designed by Lynn Forrest Architects. Erwin family collection.

Glacier Villiage IGA checkout. Erwin family collection.

Erwin's Glacier Villiage
IGA meat Case.
Erwin family collection.

Unidentified man,
above, with Vivian
Erwin, Roy DeRoux
and Charlie Robinson
in front of Glacier
Villiage IGA. Erwin
family collection.

Donna Hanna Barton, far
left, and Jerri Godwin help
customer, Jill Penworden
with her groceries at Erwin's
Glacier Village IGA. Erwin
family collection.

The crew at Glacier Villiage IGA Shortly after the opening, in Gay 90's costume. Erwin family collection. See Appendix for Jerry Rasler's list of Erwin employees, both downtown and at Erwin's Glacier Village IGA.

Jerry Rasler, Vivian Erwin, and Roy DeRoux at Super Bear in the Mendenhall Village, 1974. Jerry, Roy, Charlie Robinson, and VIvian and Marshall Erwin were owners of Glacier Villiage IGA, Inc. Erwin Family collection.

20th Century Supermarket and Foodland

Bill Cope talking to a Salesman at 20th Century Market.
Courtesy of Gary Cope.

The original Foodland Grocery, 1950's. Alaska State Library #P87-1038,
Winter & Pond collection.

Foodland Grocery checkout. Gary Paul collection.

Hub Sturrock, Co-owner, Foodland, 2004. Sue Judson collection.

Tim Whiting, 2014. Tim is the Foodland "Scribe" and co-owner up to 1995. Whiting family collection.

L-R: Unknown, Gary Paul, Dovie Choquette, Dave Adams, Ed Baker, unknown, Rick Davis, Dale Nicholas, Dewayne, Jerry Gilbertson, unknown and Tim Wolf. Gary Paul collection. Gary Paul was co-owner of Foodland until its sale in 1995 and Meat Market Manager. He is also grandson of Sam Paul, Sr, owner of Gastineau Grocery, one of Juneau's early stores, and son of "Specs Paul" a popular grocery salesman.

L-R: Dick Iverson, Blair Davis, Don Doland, and Les Caudle, Foodland Produce Dept. Gary Paul Collection.

Foodland Supermarket, 1980s. Gary Paul collection.

Thibodeau Family Stores

Joe Thibodeau, Sr. in the 1970s
Sally Thibodeau collection

Joe Thibodeau on the left, Old Home Liquor by Gold Creek, in the 1940s
Sally Thibodeau collection

Bob Thibodeau at his store, Bob's Shop-Rite Market in Douglas. Bob's interview and letters to his children are a big part of this history. Theresa Thibodeau collection.

Ken and Sally's Thibodeau's Market, 1964, before remodel. Sally Thibodeau collection.

Ken and Sally's Thibodeau's Market when it was painted brown and blue in 1965 or 1966. Sally Thibodeau collection.

Ken Thibodeau's rig in 1965. Sally Thibodeau collection.

Rainbow Foods

Rainbow Foods' Jordan Creek store, 1985. Dave Otteson collection

Dave Otteson in his office, Rainbow Foods, 1988. Dave Otteson collection

Rainbow Foods, 2nd and Seward, 1996. Dave Otteson Collection.

Rainbow Foods, 2nd and Seward Streets, 1988. Dave Otteson Collection.

Rainbow Foods, current location, 4th Street, staff photo, 2002.
Dave Otteson Collection.

Rainbow Foods, current location, 4th Street, 2007. Dave Otteson Collection.

DeHarts at Auke Bay

Sandra DeHart plays on a sled in front of the first DeHart's Grocery Store, 1940s. Sandra DeHart Meehan collection.

DeHart's, 1963. Sandra DeHart Meehan collection.

DeHart's, 1964. Jim (L) and Joe Hollingsworth, above.

Jane DeHart, right.

Sandra DeHart Meehan collection.

Hub and Dorothy Sturrock, Foodland, in retirement. Sandy Sturrock collection.

Gene and Joanne Erwin and Vivian Erwin Renshaw, 2004. Gene and Joanne were visiting while on a cruise. Erwin family collection.

The Erwin family collection of NW Coast art plaques, a gift to the Huna Heritage Foundation, April 16, 2003. L-R: Darlene Johnson, Vivian Renshaw, Marsha Bennett, and Joe Leahy. Some of these plaques can now be seen at Icy Strait Point in Hoonah. Photo by Dave Fremming.

California Grocery and Meat Market, June 2, 1940, The Daily Alaska Empire, Juneau, Alaska

George Brothers Super Market and Piggly Wiggly ads from Oct. 22, 1945, The Daily Alaska Empire, Juneau

Bert's Cash Grocery and Case Lot Grocery ads from Oct. 22, 1945, The Daily Alaska Empire, Juneau, Alaska

20th Century Super-Market ad from Feb. 16, 1949, The Daily Alaska Empire, Juneau, Alaska

20th Century Super-Market ad from May 5, 1949, The Daily Alaska Empire, Juneau, Alaska

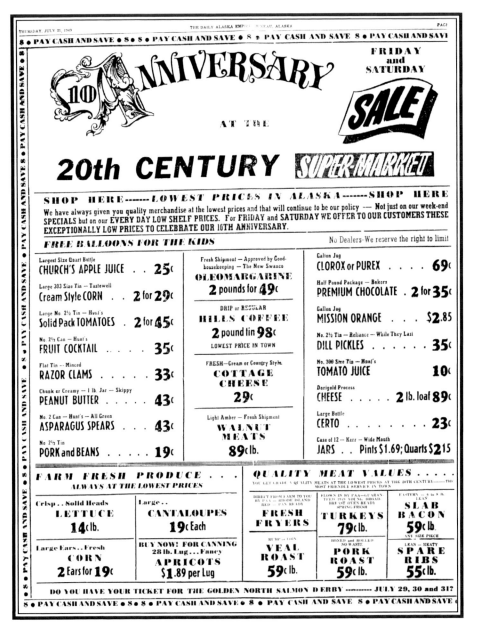

20th Century Super-Market ad from July 31, 1949, The Daily Alaska Empire, Juneau, Alaska

Case Lot Grocery ad from Nov 9, 1949, The Daily Alaska Empire, Juneau, Alaska

Home Grocery ad from Dec. 21, 1949, The Daily Alaska Empire, Juneau

Case Lot Grocery ad from Oct. 20, 1951, The Daily Alaska Empire, Juneau

Case Lot Grocery ad from Jan.2, 1967, The Daily Alaska Empire, Juneau, Alaska

FROM MOO TO YOU

Organic milk so tasty you'd think the cows were in our front yard!
Vitamins, grains, herbs, the whole shebang you'd find in a great healthy food store.

Rainbow Foods

224 Fourth Street • Juneau • 907-586-6476
www.rainbow-foods.org

DARIGOLD BUTTER
2 lbs. for $1.43

DRIP or REGULAR
HILLS COFFEE
2 pound tin 98¢
LOWEST PRICE IN TOWN

4

Young Worker's Perspective

My sister, Linda (Erwin Androes), joked about all the tricks the men who worked at Case Lot Grocery played on her when she first came to work there when she was 16. She was devoted to Esther Godkin Jokala, the head checker at Case Lot. Linda received valuable training from Esther in handling customers on the phone.

Gene Erwin also mentioned how well Esther handled customers and how much he learned from her in taking orders on the phone. Linda commented that young people were trusted with considerable responsibility and appreciated the trust they were given, a theme found in Tim Whiting's accounts of his teen years at Case Lot. Both he and Bob Thibodeau, who worked as a "swamper" at age 13, could not have worked that early [when they were that young] under current labor laws.

I talked with Donna Hanna Barton, an Erwin employee, who later was a cashier at Super Bear, working a total of 35 years for both stores. She told me several stories about her relationship with Marshall [Erwin], starting with their early history. She was a friend of his niece, Shirley. When she finally came to work for him, after years of coaxing, he took her around the store and said, "I want you to think of this store as YOUR store and the customers as YOUR customers and to treat them accordingly. All the Glacier Village box boys and checkers wanted to do their jobs that way—they all had a sense of pride in their work. And everyone looked forward to going to work there."

Since all the Erwin stores were more or less an extension of Marshall and Vivian's relationship, they both extended that line of authority throughout the organization, less so once the business incorporated. Marshall managed the over-all operation and looked to the future, Vivian was in charge of the office and finances. This created the continuity and consistency that a corporate model could rarely achieve, at least those incorporated here in Juneau. And it probably extended to the box boys and other teenagers who worked there in those early years.

Barton also joked about how often Marshall took off and "got lost and ran out of gas" so that he could have a break from the long work hours at Glacier Village. (Erwin's IGA) That Christmas the employees bought him a Gas can.

Tim Whiting's accounts of his early years at Case Lot grocery probably reflect some of the experiences of many young men who started their careers in the grocery business. Here are a few excerpts:

> The store (Case Lot Grocery) stretched from South Franklin to Marine Way and consisted of about seven narrow aisles and was about half warehouse. The initiation for every box boy in those days was to go to the bag room to get the grocery bags and restock the check stands as the store was closing. This entailed going into the warehouse, through the produce room (an aisle in the warehouse) and through the garbage room, into a side room that held the bags.
>
> The garbage room emptied out to the parking lot where the garbage trucks would pick up in the morning. There was no box crusher, no compactor and no "goat" disposal to get rid of the meat and produce trimmings. These were also stacked in the garbage room and as the store sat on pilings and fill over the waterfront, this

attracted rats--not just any rats, but the biggest rats you will ever see. The store had several cats that were good at catching mice but were seen more than once being chased by the rats. The new boxer was shown to the Bag Room and told to fill a cart up with the bags and then left alone. Having heard the rat stories and realizing you were on the far side of the garbage room with two doors between you and the main store and not very good lighting made for a very tense moment. What the older boxers didn't tell you was that the light switch for the bag room and the garbage room and the produce room was barred every night at closing. You would be just about finished getting the bag cart full and the lights would go out and you could hear the door close and the bar going across it. No more would the lights go out and the scurrying and scratching would begin with the rats moving around. PANIC??? You just think you know panic. Finding your way to the produce room door in the dark without peeing your pants was a trick, but when you realized it was barred and the only light you can see is the parking lot light shining under the garbage room door to the outside, you ran full bore into the flimsy four-by-eight-foot plywood doors and popped the lock, which was already loosened by many previous box boys.

Tim talks about bringing groceries and meats in a flatbed truck from the docks when the boats were unloaded. Here he discusses handling meat and a young man's pride in shouldering the job:

We also got beef in quarters (125 to 175 pounds) that were suspended in the meat vans from hooks. The adult meat cutters would pick them off the hooks in the van and another would put a new hook in them that had a wheel on one end. They (the meat cutters) would carry the quarter to the end of the van and place the wheel on a rail that hung from the ceiling. This rail started close to the ceiling in the warehouse and ran slightly downhill to the main aisle in the warehouse where it turned a corner. The meat was pushed on the rail to the meat department where it would go into the cooler to be cut up by the meat cutters. It was a "rite of passage" for us boxers to prove our worth by being able to carry a quarter from the van to the rail and help unload the meat van.

Gene Erwin came to work for his uncle, Marshall Erwin, when he was 17. Here is a bit of his story:

> In 1944 the world was in the throes of war. I started working in the grocery business in November 1944. I had just turned seventeen years of age and my uncle, Marshall Erwin, was in Seattle to charter the motor vessel Robert Eugene, a 125-foot packer captained by Fred Dahl, to take groceries to Juneau. The Alaska Steamship Company and Northland Marine Lines were consigned by the government to carry supplies to the interior of Alaska to build up our defenses there and southeast Alaska was low on the totem pole when it came to priority. I went north on the Robert Eugene as a deck hand and started working for the Case Lot Grocery when I arrived in Juneau….

> Those were good years, and I loved them (after talking about the late hours unloading freight and still going to work the next day). On Saturday night, after the store was locked up, we would all gather in the back room and enjoy a case of beer, which was provided by Carson Lawrence, owner of the local bakery, if we sold so much of his bread. Seems like we always got that case of beer.

Hub Sturrock:

When I was first researching grocery stores in Juneau I asked Ralph Swap (Cliff's son) about people I should talk with about the early stores. Ralph immediately mentioned Hub Sturrock. Since I didn't know him, but was a classmate of his son, Sandy, I made an appointment for the interview with both Sandy and Hub. I interviewed Hub in his home at Parkshore Condominiums.

Hub went to work for Piggly Wiggly after school while he was in high school in 1935. After graduating, he began a long career in the grocery business at Behrend's Department Store on Seward Street. When Behrend's closed the grocery, Hub started work at Home Grocery until that business sold. He then worked for California Grocery until it closed. Each time he moved the store merchandise transferred too, from Behrends to Home Grocery to California Grocery. Finally Hub began a long and successful career with Foodland, retiring as one of the owners of the busy store. Sandy Sturrock summarizes part of his dad's interview with me in 2004:

> "Hub remembered that when he started out there were no pennies. Things were priced in multiples of a nickel or dime. A pound can of pink salmon, the Happy Vale brand, was second grade to Libby's. It cost 10 cents. When the price went up, it went to two cans for 25 cents. This was the salmon they fed to the store cat(s). All the stores had them to control the chronic 'rodent' problem."

Tim Whiting talks about Hub's service at Foodland later in his career.

> Hub Sturrock had started in 1936 at the Behrend's grocery and worked up to manager. He spent fifteen years at Foodland mostly as assistant store manager. Hub carried

the bulk of the load of handling the help and the customers. He ran the store as professionally as his partners would let him. In 1980 or 1981 Hub Sturrock, the manager, who was probably the finest man I ever worked for, had a heart attack—a well- deserved heart attack.

Tim also discusses some of the circumstances that probably contributed to Hub's heart attack, including a number of partners with different ideas about how the store should run, duplicating lines of authority. Foodland was also a very busy store with substantial turnover in employees. Hub continued as an owner until he and other owners at the time (Ray Marshall and Craig Dahl) decided to sell to one owner (Rick Garrison) who then sold remaining stock in the corporation to five key employees, including Whiting.

5

Receiving Goods

Tim Whiting's tale of bringing meat to the store is only part of the story of receiving goods. Gene Erwin talks about this, too, and about long hours unloading all the groceries, which usually came in once a week on Alaska Steamship's ships. Jerry Rasler relates some of the practices Erwin's IGA used once the store opened near the airport.

Gene Erwin:

We didn't have plastic bags or Saran™ wrap then. There weren't any frozen foods. All grocery slips were totaled on mechanical adding machines. Soy sauce came in 55 gallon barrels and we collected beer bottles from the saloons and washed them and repackaged it. Many items were repacked in the store then.

Canned foods, produce, meat and milk, which was frozen, came in a single case or crate or a quarter of beef and had to be checked off the dock one at a time, loaded in the one-ton panel truck and hauled to the store. Perishable items, such as meat, produce, milk and, in the winter, anything that would freeze hard, had to be moved as soon as it was unloaded. Many times this was in the middle of the night. I can remember lots of times when the butcher and I, and sometimes the produce man, worked half the night moving freight and still had the next day to work, too."

Marshall's was the first store in Alaska to have a frozen food case, which he built by himself in the garage of his home at Norway Point. He put in the first "warm room" to ripen bananas and tomatoes and other produce. We even grew our own bean sprouts, which were bought and very much appreciated by the Filipino community. It was a different business than it is now.

Jerry Rasler:

(Erwin's Glacier Village IGA) Resupplying the stores in sufficient quantities was sometimes a problem. Everything had to be ordered two weeks in advance in order for our suppliers to get it to the steamship in Seattle and on the way to us. When it arrived it was contained in cribs ,which we collected from the dock on our flat-bed truck, four cribs at a time. Of course, if the supplier happened to be out of an item, we were just out until our next order came in. Receiving freight changed over the years. It went from cribs to containerized vans. At first our vans were delivered to Reliable Transfer. After awhile, Marshall bought us a tractor and we loaded and hauled the vans ourselves. Later the steamship company began delivering the vans to us, which was a better system.

I believe we were among the first to expand the grocery lines to non-food items. It started small and grew to quite an array of items. One item I recall in particular was children's black rubber boots with red tops. I believe every kid in Juneau had a pair.

Glacier Village (Erwin's IGA) was so far in advance of development that Marshall created a large pond and installed a huge pump to supply water for a sprinkler system.

Marlene Greenwald Johnson and Al Kookesh

Originally from Hoonah, Johnson mentioned her surprise at all the non-food items coming into Erwin's Supermarket downtown and how they added up on her grocery bill when she was a new wage earner. She also remembered her parents' early relationship with Case Lot Grocery. Her parents, who had a store in Hoonah, bought case lots of vegetables and fruits and other supplies from Case Lot Grocery. Al Kookesh of Angoon mentioned that his parents, too, bought case lots of groceries, buying in bulk, from Case Lot Grocery for their Angoon store.

I talked with both Johnson and Kookesh at our family's transfer of the IGA store Northwest Coast Native plaques which we gifted to the Icy Strait Point cruise ship facility via Huna Heritage Foundation.

Tim Whiting talks about "early freight" procedures at Foodland:

> We would get three or four … vans a week, one with meat, dairy products and some produce, the others with groceries. The best way to pack a van is to fill it up tight so things won't bounce around en route; however, in those days they would fill vans half to two-thirds full and ship them. Once in Seattle they were lifting a van off the dock onto the ship, a lift of 15-20 feet in the air. The van flipped upside down and landed on its roof from about 15 feet in the air. They just righted the van, loaded it and shipped it as is without opening the doors to check it. They did mention that the van was dropped and we should be careful opening the doors. I got the job of unloading that van and if you can imagine a half full van of ketchup, mayonnaise, mustard, vinegar, cooking oil, bleach, etc. all in glass

containers in those days being dropped from one-and-a-half stories, you get the picture. It was three weeks in those days from the time you ordered until the time the freight got there, so I spent two days after school and one Saturday picking through to find items not broken, cleaning them up and, if the labels were missing, writing what it was on the jars."

In my second or third year working, containerized cargo came into being. These containers were loaded with a crane into "liberty ships" left over from World War II and placed in the hold. The longshoremen fought containerized cargo with a vengeance.

In those days (1967) the weekly grocery ads ran from Thursday morning through Saturday night. All stores were still closed on Sunday. As we normally unloaded the weekly vans (at Foodland) on Tuesday or Wednesday and did "other duties as assigned," there was not much time to get your section up for the special days that were always the busiest. There is not a store in the Juneau area today that was as busy as Foodland was in the years 1967 through 1984 when Fred Meyer opened and even through 1995—not even close. The only way to get your job done was to come in after hours on Wednesday night and work 8 pm to midnight on your own time to be ready for the next day. Other department heads would be there most Wednesdays also. We never even thought of asking for overtime.

The biggest improvement I saw over my 30 years of being in and out of the grocery business was the benefit of competition from suppliers and freight companies servicing Juneau. This especially showed up in produce that we received. Whenever you got a bad load of produce, dairy products, etc., the stores would try to get compensation from either the supplier or the shipper. Each would claim the other was at fault. Reimbursement was almost non-existent. This changed with competition and the relaxing of upper management's insistence that you order from certain suppliers. Suppliers were anxious to guarantee products' arrival in good condition. So instead of shipping produce that was marginal or just good when it left Seattle, they [suppliers] would send the best they had and that product would survive the week of shipping.

Blend JUICE
29c

6

Light Amber — Fresh Shipment
WALNUT
MEATS
89c lb.

The Role of the Salesman

ob Thibodeau: After his initiation into his father's and John Hermle's Home Grocery, Bob worked as a salesperson. In 1940, his father purchased Totem Grocery, renaming it Thibodeau's Cash and Carry. Bob later worked with his brother, Ken, from 1954-1962. Bob operated Bob's Market in Douglas from 1963 to 1985. Here are some of his reflections on the relationship between the salesman and the stores from an interview October 27, 2005.

Bob had a produce line, MJB coffee, Carnation milk and Canadian and American meat lines. Although most food still came by boat in the '40s, Bob flew potato chips into Juneau because they were lightweight and they were fresher that way. He remembers Barney Kane, Sam "Specs" Paul, Cliff Swap and Bud Whiteside were a few of the salesmen in the 1950s and 1960s. Cliff Swap sold McCormick spices and other lines after leaving Erwin's when the downtown store closed. Bob Thibodeau also sold to restaurants like the City Café, although he mentioned he couldn't persuade Mr. Tanaka to buy MJB coffee. Bob said Mr. Tanaka bought fifteen or twenty cases of 20-pound cans of Hills Brothers coffee a month and was convinced nobody would drink MJB.

Bob comments on changes during his time as a salesman:

> "When I was a salesman, I would call on 13, 14, 15 grocery businesses. And when Kenny started to expand his grocery (1953-54), Home Grocery went out of business, Behrend's went out of business, Bert McDowell sold his

business (to Foodland), the Gastineau Grocery went out of business, Sanitary Market went out of business."

In explaining these closures Bob pointed to credit availability as the crucial factor for these small businesses:

> To get into the grocery business in the early days was easy. It didn't take too much money, and since they got credit from the wholesalers, they could give credit. But when the wholesalers started to tighten up their credit policy, then they (the small stores) couldn't give credit. They had to watch it very closely. Then the big Foodland store came along and it sucked away a lot of the business from the smaller stores—and they closed.

Bob stated that 20th Century Market refused to give credit and took out the phone so people couldn't call in orders. The store advertised lower prices due to the cash-and-carry nature of their business. They built a parking lot for the increasing number of shoppers who would drive to the supermarket, and they advertised aggressively. It was clear—the smaller, credit-oriented businesses would change or die.

Foodland continued these policies of lower prices, a big parking lot, aggressive advertising and increased selection of foods, especially meats. Tim Whiting and Gary Paul both mentioned 11-13 meat cutters working at Foodland during its busiest years. Foodland also carried a growing number of gourmet items, which they advertised often as bringing up-scale goods to loyal Juneau customers. Juneau's war-starved residents loved it.

My parents, the Erwins, put in a parking lot, but their location on South Franklin Street was not as popular as 20th Century Market's on Front and Seward. Foodland clearly had the best location, on Willoughby, within easy driving distance of downtown and Douglas residents. And Foodland had a HUGE parking lot.

My parents also incorporated, leaving behind the family partnership that had worked in the past. Eventually they moved to the airport area in 1961—considered a radical move at the time. By 1963, subdivisions in the Valley were expanding. With a seat on the Planning Commission, Marshall could see that these growing housing developments would soon need local businesses to serve them.

Determined to compete, the Erwins bought land at the corner of Glacier Highway and more recently named Shell Simmons Drive, the last parcel of Kendler's dairy farm. This location would attract both residents of the Auke Bay-Tee Harbor communities as well as families who moved into the growing subdivisions on flat lands in the Mendenhall Valley. They opened Erwin's Glacier Village IGA in 1963.

During the late 1950's, about the time of Statehood, the aggressive competition between Erwin's and Foodland spiked, as both Bill Cope and Marshall Erwin duked it out in the Wednesday newspaper ads, on radio and with give-aways including boats, dishes, pots and pans and other inducements. Erwin's Supermarket (the old Case Lot Grocery) on South Franklin Street stayed open until 1968 while the new store became better established near the airport. But the old store's market share was sinking.

Tim Whiting: Tim Whiting's career took a turn, in 1967, when he decided to change jobs. He and Marshall had had several disagreements concerning deliveries and Tim started looking for another job. He found one with Bill Cope of Foodland, but that didn't set well with Marshall. Here is Tim's version of this story:

> I applied for a job at Foodland on a Tuesday. When I went to work (at Erwin's) on Friday, I thought I should let the owner know immediately so I could

train someone else. I went into Marshall's office and told him I would be leaving at the end of two weeks and I would finish out the extra Saturday if he needed me. He asked me where I was going to work and I said Foodland. Wrong answer. He and Bill Cope had a long-standing feud as competitors and he immediately stood up and said, "Make this Saturday your last day." I immediately stood up and said, "Let's make today my last day."

Bob's sister-in-law, Sally Thibodeau, was frank about Foodland's impact on their business in her family story for *Gastineau Channel Memories*, Volume II.

Sally Thibodeau:

When Foodland opened, Ken was curious about the new store but didn't want to go into Foodland because he was afraid he might run into a customer and embarrass them. We had always written in our ads that we were a 'Super Service Store.' A large part of our business came from phone-in orders, which we would fill and deliver later that day. We never charged for this service but felt that we were at the point where we needed to charge. We thought 25 cents wouldn't be too bad. One day a woman packed her groceries from Foodland down Willoughby as far as our store. She asked Ken to deliver her groceries. Ken replied, If you've got the guts to ask me, I've got the guts to do it.' So the woman gave Ken a quarter and he delivered her groceries.

In the earlier days of credit and phone orders, Bob Thibodeau mentioned the loss of a customer was like either a death or a divorce. Bob mentioned my dad's reaction to the loss of a customer, which Bob suggested was like a death in the family.

Bob Thibodeau:

When one of your customers died, it was like a death in the family. I remember him (Marshall Erwin) coming back from a funeral and he was just devastated. Everyone guarded their own customers.

Grade U...S No. 1
POTATOES
10 lb. bag **59**¢

7

WINESAP
APPLES
5 lb. bag **89**¢

Food Shortages & Local Producers

t is hard to imagine today how critical each store and each shipment of food was to the small town of Juneau in the 1930s, 1940s and even in the 1960s. Sally Thibodeau and Tim Whiting both talk about the effect of the Foodland fire in 1963 and the panic that followed.

Sally Thibodeau:

> We were on vacation when Foodland burned. We came back right away. It was a hectic time for a town which had grown large enough to support more grocery stores to suddenly lose one.

Tim Whiting was still working for the Erwins when the fire occurred.

> One of my outstanding memories was coming to work one Saturday morning in 1963 after Foodland had burned down the night before. There were four main stores in Juneau at the time: Foodland and 20th Century owned by Bill Cope, Thibodeau's owned by Kenny Thibodeau and Erwin's Market [owned by Marshall and Vivian Erwin]. Foodland probably did the most business of any, and when it burned on a Friday night, there seemed to be a perception that the town was going to run out of groceries. We [at Erwin's market] opened at 9 am and I showed up at 8:45 am. The line [of customers] ran from the front of the store on South Franklin, through the parking lot to Marine Way and

north along Marine Way. We got one 15-minute break until we closed that night at 7:30 pm. I can remember cases of canned goods opened, priced and put on the floor in the case as no one had time to put anything on the shelf.

I remember Bill Cope coming into Erwin's Market the next week to talk to Marshall about hiring some of his box boys who were out of a job due to the fire. As far as I know, he [Cope] found jobs for every employee of Foodland either at his 20th Century Market or with other stores in town. The next week the store [Erwin's] began opening 8 am to 10 pm and opened on Sundays 9 am - 6 pm.

20th Century Market also expanded its hours until Foodland rebuilt. It was a time when Juneau's isolation and unique system of getting food was tested, and people panicked because they realized just how vulnerable the community could be.

My parents, the Erwins, often talked about another time when food was scarce. It was during the war when longshoremen and Alaska Steamship Company were fighting over containerized shipping. The longshoremen in Seattle went on strike for three months. At that time my dad and Bert McDowell, with grocers in Ketchikan, chartered the MV *Robert Eugene* to bring food to southeast Alaska customers. Gene Erwin mentioned his passage on the *Robert Eugene*, so it was 1944.

Local Producers

Nick Bavard was famous for his produce, especially the fruits and vegetables he grew in his Auke Bay garden. Hub Sturrock mentioned it and so did Bob Thibodeau. My dad, Marshall Erwin, worked for Nick during the war years when Case Lot Grocery was closed. I suspect that experience informed later Erwin produce departments, which were always lush and carefully pruned. But our compost pile at Norway Point had a steady stream of bears that loved all the wasted lettuce leaves and mushy produce too bad to sell. My sister and I picked raspberries and rhubarb from our back yard at Norway Point for sale at the store. Probably other grocers did, too. Bob Thibodeau mentioned trips to Haines for produce when he was a salesman.

As Tim Whiting discussed, shipped produce was pretty dismal until cold containers and greater competition from wholesalers became the norm. My friends loved to come to our house because we had more fresh fruit than they had at home. It was often fruit that was too ripe to sell.

Milk came frozen before temperatures remained constant in the cool vans. Many families drank canned milk or powdered milk then, others bought local dairy products. They ate canned meat like ham and Spam and canned herring, salmon and sardines, and they used canned vegetables and fruits. Remember fruit salad? And Jello? Bob Thibodeau mentioned the improvements that came with plastic bottles, especially bleach. What a mess broken bottles of bleach made, either in transit or on the grocery floor.

The "good old days" also brought excitement about Miracle Whip. A picture of my dad by a display shows how enthusiastic he was of this new idea. He and Bert McDowell combined to buy the Messerchmidt's San Francisco Bakery, located in Juneau, and tore out the ovens to put in modern ovens that could turn out Wonder bread, another new product that afforded bread at low cost to every family. It is still a mass-produced bread staple for lunches and toast. The Messerschmidts bought back their bakery after Marshall and Bert found baking was too labor intensive. They decided to leave that to the experts. Other bakeries, including the Carson Lawrence Bakery, began supplying Wonder bread to the stores, and the renamed Purity Bakery in the Messerschmidt Building regained its reputation for specialty breads, cookies and pastries. That tradition continues with newer owners at the Silverbow Bakery.

Elton Engstrom, Jr:

Another local producer in the 1930s through the 1950s was Wallis George, who owned the Coca-Cola bottling plant at the cold storage dock. Elton Engstrom, Jr, mentioned these businesses in his interview:

> [My dad] was hired to come up to Juneau in 1927. He first went to work for Sebastian Fish Company, and C. J. Sebastian was a prominent cannery operator. He bought a lot of fresh frozen fish and my dad was his agent here in Juneau, buying salmon, halibut and black cod and having it frozen. The principal owner was a man named Wallis George, who was also an owner of the Baranof Hotel, and he had many enterprises located on the dock where the cold storage was located. For instance, he was the Coca-Cola bottler and distributor. He had a bottling plant on the premises of the cold storage and at one time he had a retail fish outlet. In that sense he was an associate of the many stores in town purveying food and dry goods.

Engstrom also mentioned his own role in the local dairy business here in Juneau in the 1950s:

> I was the cleanup man for George Danner. George was in charge of the [Mendenhall] Dairy here. Eddie Nielson was the principal worker, making the ice cream. They did a lot of business. They were the principal supplier of milk [in Juneau], but, of course, that has all changed, in this case for the better, because we get better milk now.

One of the dairies operating near the Airport was The Alaska Dairy, owned by Joe Kendler. He came to Juneau from Austria in 1923. He originally bought Lee Smith's Douglas Dairy, later purchased the dairy business and ranch from Thomas Knutson, called Alaska Dairy, on Glacier Highway near the present Airport. Over the years the Kendlers supplied milk, eggs, ice cream, whipping cream and buttermilk to Juneau businesses and families. At one time they had over 100 head of cattle on their homestead.

In 1936 Juneau Dairies, Inc. was formed, consolidating Juneau Dairy owned by Lee Smith, Mendenhall Dairy owned by George Danner, Glacier Dairy owned by Frank Maier and Alaska Dairy owned by Joe Kendler. The combined herds totaled 285 animals (Willette Janes and Marie Hanna Darlin, Gastineau Heritage News, Volume 7, No. 2). The Corporation built a bottling plant at 12th Street and Glacier Highway and supplied most of Juneau's milk and ice cream through the 1950's. The building now houses the Juneau School District.

In 1961, the Kendlers sold the remaining homestead property to my parents, Marshall and Vivian Erwin. Over the years they had sold off parcels of their substantial land holdings for airport and Glacier Highway businesses. By the early 1960's air and barge shipments of milk made local dairy operations non-competitive. The Kendlers decided to sell the last of their land and moved south shortly afterward.

By the fall of 1963 the Erwins opened their new modern supermarket close to the airport on that property. Sid Smith of Juneau Dairies traded excavating of the shopping center for the old Kendler homestead, which they moved to their Mendenhall Valley property.

For more information about the Juneau dairy industry, see the Gastineau Channel Historical Society's newsletter,

Gastineau Heritage News, "Dairies on the Channel," March and June 2004, vol. 7, nos. 1 and 2, or visit the following website: www.juneau.lib.ak.us/history/documents/Juneau_Dairy_Farming_Historic_Resources_Survey_Sept_1991

8

The Supermarket comes of Age

By the late 1950's, Ken and Sally Thibodeau's grocery had morphed into a successful grocery and delicatessen business, Sally's Kitchen. They bought Home Grocery and Liquor from John Hermle and have continued in the liquor-deli business to this day, including children and grandchildren.

Marsha Erwin Bennett:

Bob Thibodeau operated Bob's Shop-Rite Market in Douglas from the 1950's to the 1970's with the help of his family. For a time Mark N Pak, operated in Lemon Creek. Spruce Market near the Douglas Bridge, DeHart's in Auke Bay and Harbor Market on 9th Street continued in business. West Juneau Cash Grocery (now Breeze-In) also operated on the Douglas side of Gastineau Channel. Now only the Breeze-In Liquor and Grocery remain to serve Douglas Island residents. The vast majority of Douglas and North Douglas folks began shopping at Foodland or Erwin's in the 1960's and adapted their shopping once the Big Box stores came to town.

The ads of the 1960's show the increasing dominance of Foodland and the struggle to compete by Erwin's Supermarket on the waterfront at South Franklin Street, Bob's Market in Douglas, Home Grocery and the remaining small groceries. At some point, the location of Foodland and its size, variety of foods and specialty meats trumped all competitors. With Erwin's move to the airport in 1963 and the closing of Erwin's Super-market downtown in 1968, Foodland's dominance only increased. Harbor Market closed and Andy and Frieda Robinson joined the Erwins at the airport. Later Vivian sold both the original IGA store at the airport and the newly built Supermarket at Mendenhall Mall (Super-bear) to Andy and Frieda's son, Charlie, who had been the accountant at the airport store and one of Erwin's partners. Robinson still owned and operated Super-Bear until his death in 2014. Now, Alaska Industrial Hardware (AIH) occupies the old supermarket space at Airport Shopping Center. The Northwest Coast Indian plaques that once adorned the grocery and its entrances were donated to Huna Heritage Foundation. Some of them are on display at Icy Strait Point in Hoonah now.

Statehood in 1959 ushered in the next phase of grocery expansion with the opening of Fred Meyer and later Costco, K-Mart and then Safeway and Wal-Mart. But our story ends with Foodland, which was sold to Alaska and Proud (A&P), an Alaska corporation in 1995. As of this writing A&P lost their lease and the Stutte's brought in a new IGA store whose owners resumed the Foodland name. Rainbow Foods continues to compete successfully on First Street near the Legislature, Courthouse and State Office buildings, as well as serving older neighbor-hoods in the hills of the original Juneau townsite. Rain-bow Foods is still owned by Dave Otteson.

My parents sold the Mendenhall Mall property to Charles Robinson and several partners after Marshall died in 1975, after Vivian and her partners opened the new store there. Our family sold Airport Shopping Center, in 2014.

This story of "creative destruction" or consolidation in the industry is not unique to Juneau of course. Both Piggly Wiggly and A & P, The Great Atlantic Tea Company, have ceased to exist after a long history of growth. In the case of A & P, Levinson relates its demise with the deaths of its founders and subsequent missteps.

People in the grocery business are used to these challenges and often shrug at the comings and goings of competitors. But they pay attention to trends. They innovate. They demand the highest standards of courtesy and service from their employees. Those who prosper listen to their customers and quickly respond to new ideas and new products. They add specialty kiosks or salad bars or cafes or bakeries, organic foods, the list goes on.

That is just the natural way of things in the grocery business.

Large Ears.. Fresh
CORN
2 Ears for **19**¢

Golden Ripe
BANANAS
25¢ lb.

9

Work Ethic & Humor

ase Lot Grocery and Glacier Village IGA probably were not the only places for pranks. In Juneau's grocery history, but I have heard these stories so often I want to share them, to show the other side of the hard work, dedication, team spirit, loyalty and other aspects of a stellar work ethic which already comes through in many of the stories you have already heard.

Vivian Erwin was a fine story teller who made people feel at ease with her humor and probably encouraged some of the pranks and jokes that were common at Case Lot. My sister, Linda, talked about some of these pranks which she experienced when she came to work at Case Lot, at 16, in 1954:

Linda Erwin Androes:

> "At that time, in 1954, the crew was like a big family. Everyone really seemed to love working there and that made it fun for me. However, since I blushed bright red at everything they loved to tease me. I think it was on my first day that I was sent on a "snipe hunt" from store to store on Franklin Street. I finally gave up and went back to the store where they all laughed their heads off.

> Another time I was called to the backroom loading deck where Bill Barron and my cousin Gene were unloading bananas. They presented me with a dead tarantula on my outstretched palm.... Every time I had occasion to stop by the meat market, the butchers would prop their locker

99

doors open so that I would have to gaze upon their pin-up girls and blush....

Vivian Erwin Renshaw as told to Marsha Erwin Bennett:

One day Vivian got into the new Erwin family car and proceeded to dent the door, which was open, on her way out of the garage. After talking about it all day with employees and customers, Vivian was on her way home. She stopped to say hello to Oliver Sarnisto, a long time employee.

When she told him about her day and the dented new car, he said "Have you seen the new snow on the mountains?" in his slow voice. From then on that phrase became an Erwin family tradition when we needed to change the subject or tone down an argument.

Case Lot always had cats because they were needed to combat the rats under the store, which was on pilings. For some time delivery men had disposed of kittens. A new delivery man who replaced George Gullefson informed Marshall that he was not going to drown any kittens. He suggested Marshall do it. Marshall couldn't do it either. So Marshall devised the "Case Lot Kitten Deal" which lasted for many years—6 cans of cat food with every kitten you take home. They gave away over 100 kittens.

Donna Hanna Barton:

Donna told me about Bill Barron's peanut story—a time when Vivian acted on a habit Bill had of picking up peanuts from an open barrel on his way out on a delivery run. She tied a number of peanuts together on a string so that the peanuts trailed after Bill, much to his embarrassment, and everyone else's chuckles.

Donna told a story on Marshall too, at Glacier Village IGA. The crew was convinced that Marshall intentionally ran out of gas often so that he could get a break from the intense, fast pace of the new store. So at Christmas they bought him a gas can.

Another time, Donna mentioned that a clerk at the new drug store wondered who the man in the Pendleton shirt was who kept coming into their store, looking around and then leaving without buying anything. Donna said, "Oh that is Marshall Erwin, the owner of Glacier Village IGA. He is probably just getting ideas from looking at your displays."

Pioneer Grocers: Summary and Conclusions

Juneau was founded during the Gold Rush of the 1890's and continued as a small mining and fishing town into the 1940's. Houses and businesses hugged the hills. Miners and fishermen were the lifeblood of the town. South Franklin Street, formerly the staging area for the Gold Rush, was a lively theater for grocers, fishermen and their boats, bars and a Red Light District. Front Street, Seward Street and Willoughby Avenue each had their share of neighborhood groceries, bakeries and other businesses. A few professional families, Territorial government employees and their families, cannery and local business clerks or restaurant employees catered to the small population.

Grocery families started coming to Juneau from Europe, starting in 1887, with B.M. Behrends, who came from Germany. Behrends came to Juneau, via Sitka, in 1887. He founded businesses in Skagway and Fairbanks as well serving the Gold Rush miners, hangers-on and occasional spouses, who flooded Alaska at the turn of the century searching for gold. Later he founded B. M. Behrends Bank, built the Department store and grocery, which would continue, in a new concrete building on Seward Street until its closing in 1980. (GM, VI,20)

Joe Thibodeau and Gus Messerschmidt came to Juneau in 1914. Joe worked at St. Ann's Hospital until he joined forces with John Hermle to found Home Grocery on Willoughby Avenue. (GM, VII,384). Gus Messerschmidt founded San Francisco Bakery in 1899 after arriving here from Germany. The bakery, and concrete building it housed continued in Messerschmidt family hands until 1980. (GM, VI, 331)

The Goldstein family, Charles, Izzy (Isadora) and Belle Goldstein Simpson, all had important businesses in Juneau. Their father, Charles, had been a major supplier to the Gold Rush trade, coming originally from Russia via Germany. Charles Jr. built a concrete building on Seward Street which housed a number of groceries over the years. He was a fur trader in the early days. Izzy had a fishing and mining supply store operator on South Franklin Street. Belle Simpson owned The Nugget Shop in several locations. It was one of the earliest and most successful tourist shops in downtown Juneau. Charles Goldstein also owned the building on South Franklin Street which he later sold to Marshall and Vivian Erwin, my parents, who founded Case Lot Grocery there in 1938. The Goldstein family still owns several Juneau properties managed locally.

Hub Sturrock, John Hermle, Bob and Ken Thibodeau were second generation Juneau folks prior to their grocery careers. Bill Cope, Marshall and Vivian Erwin, Bert McDowell, Frieda and Andy Robinson, Jane and Jim DeHart all came to Juneau in the 1930's or early 1940's. Hard times in the Dust Bowl or unemployment or underemployment during the Great Depression pushed these families north. During the 1930's many of these migrants opened groceries. Dozens of stores dotted the streets of this early settlement. Each had a few customers, gave them credit and delivered their groceries up the hills, stairs and roads of the early town. At night they served on City Councils or as volunteer firemen, like the founders of Juneau before them.

The standard of living in Juneau prior to the end of World War II, in 1945, was not so different from small towns across America. One newspaper and regular passenger ships and a few airplanes brought the news and goods to Juneau. Most families did not own a car. They cooked at home, went to an occasional movie, hunted and fished for their daily meals. A piano at home, church or school, basketball and baseball, hiking and picnicking near the Mendenhall Glacier or swimming in the Evergreen Bowl occupied their children.

A surge of change occurred once World War II ended in 1945. Suddenly war time manufacturing turned to refrigerators and washing machines, and later TVs. Transportation became more reliable, ushering in a wider variety of foods along with home appliances, cars and building materials. Roads built in war-time helped this trend.

As cars and building materials became more accessible, homes were built outside the tight footprint of the early town. Homes in Casey-Shattuck subdivision and out the Glacier Highway and Douglas Highway became more common. Grocers and other businesses followed the trend toward decentralization. As the Territorial Government expanded, more white collar workers came to Juneau. Over time City, Territorial and later State government employees came to dominate the town. The Coast Guard headquartered here. The University was founded and expanded. NOAA and the Forest Service grew.

In 1945 20th Century Market opened on Front and Seward Street. It was the first "cash and carry supermarket" in Juneau. Like larger stores in communities across America, this new concept in grocery trade threatened the old style of small businesses which depended on a small number of loyal customers, credit and delivery. Over the course of about 10-15 years virtually all the small stores that operated in Juneau in the 1930's and 1940's had either closed, sold out to larger stores or re-organized to meet the challenge.

Containerized cargo in 1953 jump-started the grocery wars of the 1950's and early 1960's. Food choices, grocery store sizes and fierce competition brought prices down for Juneau customers and variety and quality of foods soared.

By the late 1950's Foodland on Willoughby, Erwin's Supermarket on South Franklin, Thibodeau's on Willoughby and

20th Century Market on Front Street dominated the grocery trade. Once Foodland expanded and prospered, 20th Century closed, Thibodeau's began specializing in delicatessen and liquor and eventually Erwin's Supermarket moved to the expanding Mendenhall Valley at the Airport, to serve customers there, and they closed their South Franklin store.

Another wave of change in groceries came once Statehood, in 1959, pushed Juneau's population higher adding a growing State bureaucracy and their families to the town. Federal and City governments grew too, as the State economy grew, Native Land Claims were settled in 1971 and the Prudhoe Bay Oil fields came on line. Lobbyists for the Oil Companies and other interests and non-profits and attorneys and professionals filled the old Apartment buildings in the downtown area. Native Corporations and non-profit enterprises grew to meet the health, welfare and educational needs of their shareholders.

First Fred Meyer, an Oregon-based chain opened along Glacier Highway (in 1983). Then Costco from Seattle, built their warehouse store in a new area near Lemon Creek. K-Mart followed. Carr's Safeway came to the corner of Egan Drive and Riverside Drive in the Mendenhall Valley, near SuperBear, a local store. Fred Meyer doubled in size to meet the Wal-Mart Challenge in early 2006. By then Foodland had sold to an Alaskan chain, Alaskan and Proud in 1995. Wal-Mart took over the K-Mart building in Lemon Creek in the fall of 2007.

These large grocery and general merchandise stores dominate the suburbs of Juneau now, as they do suburban malls and cross-roads across America. Smaller businesses struggle in Malls along Glacier Highway, downtown and in Lemon Creek. Jordon Creek and Mendenhall Malls now cater to community offices and restaurants, with ever fewer retail businesses. Today, Nugget Mall and Airport Shopping Center on Glacier Highway and Grants Plaza in Lemon Creek continue serving customers in many retail shops, most locally owned, a few representing national retail chains. Downtown South Franklin Street and side streets have come to be dominated by Cruise ship stores in summer, with a dwindling number of local businesses staying open in winter.

Like cities all over America, Juneau activists are pushing to revitalize the downtown core, long eroded by government expansion and declining retail vitality. A new Museum Archives and Library building, now under construction near the waterfront, will one day contribute to that revitalization. The Willoughby Avenue neighborhood of Foodland in the 1950's and 1960's is another area likely to host a new urban expansion tied in with the growth of the Arts District forming around the Museum-Archives-Library and future Performing Arts Center.

The forces driving change in Juneau now won't affect grocers as much as in the past. Tourism, mining, resource development and a thriving University and Federal research culture are the drivers of local change now, along with State and local government. The huge "big box" stores of the present will expand to meet the challenges of increased population, diversified businesses and employment. Their organizational structure, supply chains and international scope suggest that they will weather whatever demands come their way in Juneau. How well smaller businesses survive is not so certain.

Bibliography: Works Cited

Books

DeArmand, R.N., *Old Gold: A Collection of Historical Vignettes, KINY,* Juneau, Alaska, No date.

DeArmand, R.N., The Founding of Juneau, Juneau: Gastineau Channel Centennial Association, 1967.

Humphrey, Kim, *Shelf Life: Supermarkets and the Changing Cultures of Consumption,Cambridge: Cambridge University Press, 1998.*

Janes, Willette, Draft Report of the Juneau Dairy Farming Historic Resources Survey, Juneau: City and Borough of Juneau, 1991.

Employee's Manual: Erwin's Supermarket, A Family of Friendly People, Juneau, Alaska, January, 1962.

Kendler, Mathilde, *Kendler's: The Story of a Pioneer Alaska Juneau Dairy,* Northwest Publishing Co, 1983.

Levinson, Marc, *The Great A & P and the Struggle for Small Business in America, New* York, Hill and Wang, 2011.

Pioneer Book Committee, *Gastineau Channel Memories*, Volume I: 1880 – 1959, Juneau, Alaska, 2001. Grocery family histories in this volume include:

Nick and Mary Bavard – California Grocery, p. 35

Jim and Jane DeHart – DeHart's Grocery, p. 128

Marshall and Vivian Erwin – Case Lot Grocery, Erwin's Supermarket, Erwin's Glacier Village IGA, pp. 145-46

Chuck Freymiller – 20th Century Market, p. 162-63

Thomas George – George Brothers Market, Leader Department Store, p. 168-69

Goldstein family – pp. 177-78

Hermle – Home Grocery, pp. 221-22

McDowell, Betty – Bert's Cash Grocery, p. 319

Messerschmidt, George and Amy – San Francisco Bakery, Purity Bakery, pp. 331-335

Nygard – Harbor Market, pp. 365-36

Olds, John, by Donna Hanna Barton – Erwin's and Superbear, pp. 370-71

Paul, Sam Jr. – Gastineau Grocery, p. 396

Robinson, Andy and Frieda – Harbor Market and Erwin's Glacier Village IGA, pp.450-51

Soufalis, James and Elsie N. – Star Bakery, pp.477-78

Swap, Clifford and Edna – Case Lot Grocery, pp. 493-94

Whiting, Gene and Geraldine, by Tim Whiting – Case Lot Grocery, Erwin's Supermarket, Foodland, pp. 401-04

Pioneer Book Committee, *Gastineau Channel Memories: 1880-1967, Volume II,* Juneau, Alaska, Alaska Litho, 2004. Grocery family histories in this volume include:

Behrends, B. M. and Virginia Pakle – BM Behrend's Bank and Department Store and Grocery, pp. 20-21

Hermle, Jack Jr. – Home Grocery, p. 131

Thibodeau, Ken and Sally – Thibodeau's Grocery and Sally's Kitchen, pp. 384-87

Whiting, Gene and Geraldine, by Tim Whiting – Case Lot Grocery, Erwin's Supermarket, Foodland, pp. 401-04

Pioneer Book Committee, *Gastineau Channel Memories: 1880-1967, Volume III,* Juneau, Alaska, Alaska Litho, 2008. Grocery family histories in this volume include:

Rosenberger, Smokey and Betty – Foodland, pp. 279-280

Thibodeau, Bob and Ril – Bob's Shop-Rite Market, Douglas, pp. 318-320

Juneau Cold Storage, pictures and commentary, pp. 355-56

Daniel A. Seiver and Susan R. Fison, Alaska Population Growth , 1960-1973, ISER, Fairbanks, University of Alaska, April, 1975.

Stone, David and Brenda, Hard Rock Gold, Juneau: Centennial Committee, 1980.

Territory of Alaska, Telephone Directory, March, 1952, Alaska Telephone Corp.

Trillin, Calvin, *Messages From My Father*, New York, The Noonday Press, 1996.

U.S. Bureau of Labor Statistics, U. S. Department of Labor, "100 Years of U.S. Consumer Spending, Washington, D.C., May, 2006, Report 991.

Interviews and Story Submissions

Hub Sturrock – December 1, 2004 Interview by Marsha Bennett

Elton Engstrom – July 1, 2006 interview by Marsha Bennett

Donna Hanna Barton – telephone interview, January 14, 2005

Bob Thibodeau – October 27, 2005 interview by Marsha Bennett

Tim Whiting autobiography – October, 2005 - Submission

John Hermle Jr. – August 3, 2005 interview by Marsha Bennett

Jerry Rasler – Email submissions, January and August, 2006

Gene Erwin – "My Grocery Story"- August 6, 2005 - Submission

Linda Erwin Androes – "Reflections"- Submission, 2006

Vivian Erwin Renshaw – History of the Erwin Building, no date

Dave Otteson, "Rainbow Foods: A Personal History" - 2006 Submission,

KINY, "Our Town" Radio Program: The Grocery Business with Jane MacKinnon, Bob Thibodeau, Vivian Renshaw and Clancy Foster – March 23, 1992

Magazine and Newspaper Articles

Andree, Kim. "Community Stomping Ground: Tennis Champ Remembers History Of Evergreen Bowl – Cope Park." Juneau Empire. August 16, 2009. C1.

Andree, Kim. "A Name Known to Many." (Bob Thibodeau) Juneau Empire. January 17, 2010. C1.

Marsha Erwin Bennett, Norway Point Memories, Part II. Gastineau Heritage News October 2002: 4-5.

Blackwell, Mike. "Front Street – Then and Now." Gastineau Heritage News, February, 2000.

Boddy, Doug. "Clearing Up Errors in Cope Park Article." Juneau Empire, August 19, 2009. A7.

Rachel Bowlby. "Carried Away: The Invention of Modern Shopping. Progressive Grocer survey.

Christine Crooks, China Joe and other Foreign Miners, Juneau: Gold Rush Stories, Gold Rush Centennial Task Force, State of Alaska, 1999.

Daily Alaska Empire. "New Foodland Supermarket to Open in Juneau." August 24, 1955.

Daily Alaska Empire. "Case Lot Grocery Becomes Erwin's Supermarket." January16, 1957.

Daily Alaska Empire Extra. "Erwin's Observes Birthday. January 15, 1958.

Janes, Willette. Dairies on the Channel, Part 1. Gastineau Heritage News. March, 2004.

Janes, Willette and Marie Hanna Darlin. Dairies on the Channel, Part II. Gastineau Heritage News. June, 2004.

Juneau Empire. Dairy Days, Inside. January 9, 2000.

Juneau Empire. "Our History Through the Decades: A Special Celebrate 2000 Publication. Fall/Winter, 1999.

Erickson, Gregg. "Juneau Weathered Well During Great Depression." Juneau Empire. February 10, 2008.

Gerbi, Mary Lou. "The Goldstein Family Legacy. Alaskan Southeaster. November, 2000: 18-19.

Martin, Andrew. "Miles of Aisles for Milk? Not Here. New York Times. September 10, 2008.

McPhee, John. "Structure." The New Yorker. January 14, 2013: 46-55.

Morrison, Eric. "June 30 Marks Historical Day in Alaska Statehood." Juneau Empire. June 30, 2008.

Obituary: Herman (Smokey) Jacob Rosenberger. Juneau Empire. November 24, 2006.

Obituary: Eva Mae Nygard. Juneau Empire. March 20, 2002

Websites

www.allbusiness.com

Buyers Top 25 Dollar Retailers, Private Label Buyers, July, 2003.

www.juneau.org/parksrec/Museum/digitalbob

August 28, 1914 – "Five Concrete Buildings being built in Juneau"

March 20, 1934 – "Mike Pusich combines meats, groceries and general merchandise in The Hub in Douglas"

March 31, 1937 – "The Home Grocery...is being enlarged to twice its Size. Owners John Hermle and Joe Thibodeau also operate American Meat On Front Street."

May 3, 1937 – Sam Paul's Gastineau Grocery Moved to its new location"

May 12, 1947 – Sale of California Grocery and Market."

July 1, 1947 – "Harbor Market changed hands."

www.pigglywiggly.com: About us.

www.progressivegrocer.com/research

www.wholefoodsmarket.com: Company History, July 10, 2006.

www.wholefoodsmarket.com: John Mackey's Blog: An Open Letter to Michael Pollan. June 20, 2006.

Library Collections

Alaska State Library, Historical Collection: China Joe, 1834-1917, "China Joe" papers, 1917-2004, MS217.

www.juneau.lib.ak.us/community/history/junohist.htm: The Founding of Juneau, Alaska by Nancy Ferrell, 2008.

Appendix
Clusters of Food Retailers in the Juneau Area

Seward Street - North Franklin - Front Street

1881   Northwest Trading Company

1891   B. M. Behrend's Department Store (general merchandise and food), Seward & Third streets

1894   Juneau Bakery
Juneau Meat Market

1899   San Francisco Bakery (became Purity Bakery), Second & Seward streets

1900   California Bakery, Front Street
Blomgren's Market, Front Street

1908   Alaska Meat Company (became Sanitary Meats)

1914   Clare Brothers' Grocery (formerly Reliable Grocery), Front Street

1920   Billy Taylor's candy store (formerly China Joe's), Main Street

1920s Washington Cooperative, Fourth & Main streets

1925   Garnick's, Seward Street, across from Behrend's

1927   Frye-Bruin Meat Company, Front Street, Maloney Building

1928   Piggly Wiggly, Front Street, Percy Reynold's building

1928   Belmont Grocery (former Winter and Pond Studio) Front Street

1929   D J Castros, Seattle Fruit and Produce, Front Street

1930 United Food, Seward Street, Goldstein Building

1937 Gastineau Grocery, Front Street, across from 20th Century Super Market

1937 Irving's Grocery, Front Street, Lewis Building

1942 Bert's Cash Grocery, Seward Street, next to Behrend's

1945 20th Century Super Market, Front & Seward streets

1950s Owl Grocery

1980s Rainbow Foods, Seward Street

Willoughby Avenue to Douglas Bridge

1916 McCoy's

1916 Henry Hansen grocery

1929 Home Grocery (also meats, liquor), Willoughby at Gold Creek

1930s Jim Ellen's Grocery

Corner "Cottage" Grocery

1933 Totem Grocery (became Irving's Food and Liquor)

1933 Carr's Grocery

1933 Juneau Grocery

1935 Bert McDowell's first store

1936 Parker's Market

1940s Star Value

1942 Nygard's Market

1950s Carson Lawrence's Bakery

1950s Glover's Spruce Grocery and Sturm Lockers

1950 Stevenson's Market

1935 Joe Thibodeau's Market

1953 Foodland

1953 Thibodeau's Market and Sally's Kitchen

South Franklin - Dock Area

1883 R. Goldstein
      Swanson Brothers

1894 The Baker

1900 Izzy Goldstein fishery supply and grocery

1917 George Brothers

1931 Star Bakery

1931 California Grocery

1938 Case Lot Grocery

1950s Spudnut Shop and Bakery

1951 Juneau Cold Storage, deli, fishermen's supplies

1960s Kenny's Fountain and grocery

Other Area Grocery Stores, a Partial Listing

1908 George Brothers (first store), Douglas

1930 Roscoe's (became DeHart's), Auke Bay

1953 Bob's Shop-Rite Market, Douglas

1953 West Juneau Cash Grocery (became Breeze-In)

1964 Erwin's Glacier Village IGA (became Shop N Kart), Airport area

1960s Mark N Pak, Lemon Creek

1960s Fred Meyer, Egan Drive

1970s Mendenhall Village IGA (became Super Bear), Mendenhall Mall

1990s Costco, Lemon Creek

1990s Kmart, Lemon Creek

Breeze-In, Egan Drive, Valley, West Juneau and Lemon Creek

2007 Walmart

Sources: Alaska State Library, Vivian Erwin Renshaw, Marie Darlin, Hub Sturrock, newspaper accounts, Digital Bob files from the Juneau-Douglas City Museum. Differences between this listing of stores and those in Hub Sturrock's list (page 14), highlight the large number of food stores which Juneau has hosted.

Jerry Rasler's List of Erwin Employees, Downtown

Cliff Swap, store manager, prior to closing the downtown store

Bob Dapcevich, delivery stocker

Oliver Sarnisto, frozen foods

Don Dungan, produce

Jenny ------ produce

Esther Jockala, checker

Roy DeRoux, stocker, later partner at Glacier Village IGA

Ken Scott, freight, stocker

Lucille Pyle, office

Frieda Robinson, office

Betty Marks, checker

Donna Hanna, checker

Alice Dubber, checker

Andy Cadiente, stocker, produce

Bill Johnson, Meat Market Manager

Russ Jones, meat cutter

Al Cottie, meat cutter

Jim Campbell, meat cutter

Kay Wright, meat wrapper

Bert Bertholl, meat cutter

Walt Burkhart, freight, stocker

Jack Woods, freight, stocker

Jerry White, delivery

Hank Hines, meat cutter

Geri Goodwin, checker

Ellen Hunt, checker

Vern Roberts, produce

Dennis Cunningham, produce

Roger Lee, meat cutter

Rod Selvig, meat cutter

Russ Stevenson, stocker

Art Sanford, freight, stocker

Ethel Gelineau

Later at Glacier Village

Charlie Robinson, Partner, office

Marvin Dindinger

Dennis Green, produce

Mike Overman, delivery

Dianne DeRoux